Haruki Murakami and His Early Work

Haruki Murakami and His Early Work

The Loneliness of the Long-Distance Running Artist

Masaki Mori

LEXINGTON BOOKS
Lanham • Boulder • New York • London

Published by Lexington Books
An imprint of The Rowman & Littlefield Publishing Group, Inc.
4501 Forbes Boulevard, Suite 200, Lanham, Maryland 20706
www.rowman.com

6 Tinworth Street, London SE11 5AL, United Kingdom

Copyright © 2021 The Rowman & Littlefield Publishing Group, Inc.

All rights reserved. No part of this book may be reproduced in any form or by any electronic or mechanical means, including information storage and retrieval systems, without written permission from the publisher, except by a reviewer who may quote passages in a review.

British Library Cataloguing in Publication Information Available

Library of Congress Cataloging-in-Publication Data Available

Library of Congress Control Number: 2020950633

ISBN 978-1-7936-3597-6 (cloth : alk. paper)
ISBN 978-1-7936-3599-0 (pbk : alk. paper)
ISBN 978-1-7936-3598-3 (electronic)

*To My Mother,
And My Father in Memoriam*

Contents

Foreword		ix
Acknowledgments		xvii
1	Murakami's Self-Conscious Ambivalence as a Japanese Writer	1
2	Beyond National Canonicity: Murakami and the Japanese Literary Canon	7
3	Translation as a Beneficial Diversion for Murakami's Fiction Writing	13
4	"The Second Bakery Attack": The Induced Burial of Young Aspirations	19
5	"The Elephant Vanishes": What Efficiency Produces	39
6	"TV People": The Slick Assault by Electronic Media	57
7	Televisual Appropriation and Fear in "TV People" and *Ringu*	77
Afterword		85
Appendix: Works by Murakami Haruki		89
Bibliography		101
Index		109
About the Author		115

Foreword

Let me start with enumerating elements of 村上春樹 Murakami Haruki's life as I consider them relevant to my argument. On January 12, 1949, he was born in Kyoto, Japan, as the only child to his parents. They were both schoolteachers of Japanese. The family soon moved to the port city of Kobe, and Murakami lived there until he graduated from high school and studied for the college entrance examinations for another year. He tends not to say much about his childhood or his family.[1] There are a few notable facts about the early part of his life, however. Born more than three years after the end of World War II, he did not directly experience the devastation of war. His father was a war veteran and a son of a Buddhist monk, and the boy Murakami grew up watching him praying for the war dead in a daily practice. As a teenager who was appreciative of neither his parents' academic specialization nor the educational system, Murakami read Western literature in translation while learning to read English paperback books left by foreign sailors at used bookstores in the port city. He was also greatly interested in world history, reading books on the subject regularly.

Murakami moved to Tokyo in 1968 and entered Waseda University, majoring in Theater and Film. He was not a diligent student, partly because that year saw the rise of the second wave of vehement student-led demonstrations against the renewal of the Japan-U.S. Security Treaty, and he initially joined the movement. He soon quit, disillusioned with his fellow demonstrators' insincerity about a revolutionary objective that ultimately failed. He did not turn to classes for formal education anyway. Instead, he watched films in movie theaters or read film scripts in the university's theater museum. He later stated that the only good thing that happened during his college days was to meet his future wife Yoko. They got married in 1971.

It took Murakami seven years to graduate from the university in 1975. His thesis for graduation was titled "*Amerika eiga ni okeru tabi no keifu* アメリカ映画における旅の系譜 (The Genealogy of Travels in American Cinema)." While still enrolled the previous year, he started a jazz café and bar called Peter Cat with his wife in Tokyo. In spite of some financial difficulties, Peter Cat was a success in the end, largely owing to his hard work. The clientele flocked to the bar where he played his favorite records and provided young jazz musicians with performance opportunities.

Taking time off from managing the jazz bar one afternoon in April 1978, he was watching a professional baseball game of an almost perpetual underdog team called the Yakult Swallows, which he supported. While he lay drinking beer on the outfield bleachers' lawn of the Tokyo stadium, he suddenly felt a kind of epiphanic drive to write a novel. He started writing a draft, using the kitchen table after working hours. He was dissatisfied with the first outcome, and he ventured to translate one chapter into English first, and then back into Japanese. Although he was self-admittedly far from having a solid command of the English language at that time, he thereby acquired his own narrating voice, and the attempt resulted in his first novel, *Kaze no uta wo kike* 風の歌を聴け (*Hear the Wind Sing*) (1979). The novel brought him his first literary prize.

Murakami's novels in the 1980s also include *1973 nen no pinbōru* 1973年のピンボール (*Pinball, 1973*) (1980), *Hitsuji wo meguru bōken* 羊をめぐる冒険 (*A Wild Sheep Chase*) (1982), *Sekai no owari to hādoboirudo wandārando* 世界の終りとハードボイルド・ワンダーランド (*Hard-Boiled Wonderland and the End of the World*) (1985), and *Dansu Dansu Dansu* ダンス・ダンス・ダンス (*Dance Dance Dance*) (1988). They had a modest success in Japan. A breakthrough came with the publication of *Noruwei no mori* ノルウェイの森 (*Norwegian Wood*) in 1987, when Murakami was away in Greece and Italy during the latter half of the 1980s to avoid troublesome contact with the literary establishment back home. He initially could not believe that his novel became a best seller. He also stayed away from Japan when he was invited to Princeton University in the early 1990s and wrote two novels, including *Kokkyō no minami, taiyō no nishi* 国境の南、太陽の西 (*South of the Border, West of the Sun*) (1992) and *Nejimaki-dori kuronikuru* ねじまき鳥クロニクル (*The Wind-Up Bird Chronicle*) (1994, 1995). Around the mid-1990s, Murakami began to be recognized internationally and has now become popular in many parts of the world.

In addition to *Hard-Boiled Wonderland and the End of the World*, *Norwegian Wood*, *Dance Dance Dance*, and *The Wind-Up Bird Chronicle*, Murakami has published three more multivolume novels in Japan to date, including *Umibe no Kafuka* 海辺のカフカ (*Kafka on the Shore*) (2002), *Ichi-kyū-hachi-yon*

1Q84 (2009, 2010), and *Kishidanchō goroshi* 騎士団長殺し (*Killing Commendatore*) (2017). He has other kinds of publications, such as single-volume novels, collections of short stories, travel journals, essays on various topics, and translations. In addition to the ones mentioned above, his single-volume novels include *Supūtoniku no koibito* スプートニクの恋人 (*Sputnik Sweetheart*) (1999), *Afutā dāku* アフターダーク (*After Dark*) (2004), and *Shikisai wo motanai Tazaki Tsukuru to, kare no junrei no toshi* 色彩を持たない多崎つくると、彼の巡礼の年 (*Colorless Tsukuru and His Years of Pilgrimage*) (2013).

Some of Murakami's short stories have a serious content, while others are obviously meant to be light-heartedly entertaining. Among the collections of his short stories worth mentioning are *Hotaru, naya wo yaku, sono ta no tanpen* 螢・納屋を焼く・その他の短編 (*Fireflies, Barn Burning, and Other Short Stories*) (1984), *Pan'ya saishūgeki* パン屋再襲撃 (*The Second Bakery Attack*) (1986), *TV pīpuru* TVピープル (*TV People*) (1990), *Rekishinton no yūrei* レキシントンの幽霊 (*The Ghosts of Lexington*) (1996), *Kami no kodomo-tachi wa mina odoru* 神の子どもたちはみな踊る (*All God's Children Dance*) (2000), *Tokyo kitan shū* 東京奇譚集 (*Strange Tales of Tokyo*) (2005), and *Onna no inai otoko-tachi* 女のいない男たち (*Men Without Women*) (2014).

As an avid traveler, Murakami has visited many corners of the world, sometimes sojourning in a place for an extended period. As a result, he has written several travel journals or essays. A typical example is *Yagate kanashiki gaikokugo* やがて哀しき外国語 (*The Foreign Language That Makes Us Sad Before Long*) (1994) in which he observes and sometimes critiques aspects of American society based on his stay in the United States in the early 1990s. He has also published a number of nonfictional books on his other serious pastimes, especially running and music. He regularly has runs, including daily jogging early in the morning, mid-distance practice in preparation for competitive long-distance races, and participation in marathons and triathlons, often outside of Japan. *Hashiru koto ni tsuite kataru toki ni boku no kataru koto* 走ることについて語るときに僕の語ること (*What I Talk about When I Talk about Running*) (2007), titled after Raymond Carver's short story, focuses on his various running experiences around the world, including a midsummer run on the original Marathon route in Greece.

Murakami's other passion is music, including jazz, rock, and classical music. Over the years, he has collected a huge amount of records and CDs. He sometimes listens to music casually, such as listening to rock pieces on a portable device while jogging. His listening attitude, however, is usually much more intense, as a result of which he has acquired a deep appreciation and understanding of the three kinds of music and almost a professional insight into them. In addition to short essays, he has published several books on music, illustrated by *Ozawa Seiji-san to, ongaku ni tsuite hanashi wo suru* 小澤征爾さんと、音楽について話をする (*Talking about Music with Mr. Ozawa Seiji*) (2011) in which he discusses classical music on an equal footing with the internationally renowned principal conductor of the Boston Symphony Orchestra.

Translation from English is akin to a devoted hobby for Murakami, and he has established himself as a major translator of modern works, mainly from twentieth-century American literature. Some pieces are new introductions into the Japanese language, while he made anew his own versions of existing translations by others. Representative examples, which reflect his personal tastes and preferences, include *The Catcher in the Rye* by J. D. Salinger, *The Great Gatsby* by F. Scott Fitzgerald, and *The Long Goodbye* by Raymond Chandler. The complete works of Raymond Carver offer another instance. Murakami admits to insufficient proficiency to translate from any other foreign language than English. Through reading translation, however, he has become extensively familiar with Western literature in general. The two novelists whom he often mentions as objects of his great admiration are Fyodor Dostoevsky and Franz Kafka.

Murakami has penned other kinds of publications. *Murakami Haruki, Kawai Hayao ni aini iku* 村上春樹、河合隼雄に会いにいく (*Murakami Haruki Goes to Meet Kawai Hayao*) (1996) records his dialogues with a renowned scholar of psychotherapy. The voluminous *Andāguraundo* アンダーグラウンド (*Underground*) (1997) collects his sixty-one interviews with some of the survivors of the sarin nerve gas attack on the Tokyo subway system on March 20, 1995, as his reaction to the incident itself, the religious cult that caused it, and the nature of Japanese society. *Wakai dokusha no tame no tanpen shōsetsu annai* 若い読者のための短編小説案内 (*A Guide to Short Stories for Young Readers*) (1997) is based on the lectures on six modern Japanese writers that he gave at Princeton and Tufts Universities. He has also written several books on the topics of translation and his self-awareness as a novelist. Additionally, he has a number of books and CD-ROMs that record his correspondence with his readers through a temporary website.

Overall, Murakami has proven himself a prolific, popular writer of his time. As a result, he has been awarded international literary prizes in addition to several domestic ones. For instance, although he is usually averse to public and media exposure at home, he chose to accept the Franz Kafka Prize in 2006 to express his sincere respect for the Czech writer. In 2009, he caused a controversy with his acceptance speech for the Jerusalem Prize when he stated his moral support for the eggs that are thrown against the wall as a metaphor of helpless peoples who resist systematic oppression. In 2011, Murakami donated the monetary prize of the International Catalunya Prize to the victims of the tsunami and earthquake that struck Japan earlier the same year. Other distinctions include the World Fantasy Award (2006), the Frank O'Connor International Short Story Award (2006), the Welt Literature Award (2014), and the Hans Christian Andersen Literature Award (2016), as well as honorary doctoral degrees from the University of Liège (2007), Princeton University (2008), the University of Hawaii (2012), and Tufts University (2014).

Over the years, media and bookmakers have consistently mentioned Murakami's name as one of the top possible recipients of the Nobel Prize for Literature every fall before the Selection Committee announced the actual awardee. He has not had the honor as yet. He considers the entire clamor about him troublesome and hampering to his writing profession.

When I read *Hard-Boiled Wonderland and the End of the World* in 2003, I recognized an imaginative capacity, originality, and construction far different from and beyond the confines of modern Japanese literature. It was a fresh surprise, all the more so because I was familiar with some of his earlier novels. Since then, I have mainly directed my research interest at Murakami's writings. The current monograph is the first result of my studies that stretch across two decades and an ocean, aiming at a holistic understanding of Murakami Haruki as an artist dedicated to his profession. Here, my objective is to examine his non-novelistic activities and writings, particularly through the lens of some of his early, most important short stories and nonfictional pieces.

Partly because of his individual preferences, partly due to his strategic choice as a writer, Murakami's writings are so full of references to Western cultural and consumer items that it is often hard to find distinctively Japanese counterparts for many pages apart from the original language used. As a result, readers outside Japan who read his novels in translation can easily identify with his characters and often regard his fictional settings as not particularly Japanese. His personal lifestyle, as he frequently visits and stays abroad and tends to prefer Western products, confirms his apparent lack of cultural self-identity as Japanese. Thus, the first three chapters of this monograph are dedicated to the aesthetic issues that arise from an artist's cultural hybridity. In chapter 1: "Murakami's Self-Conscious Ambivalence as a Japanese Writer," I discuss the ambiguity of Murakami's cultural identity, arguing that such ambiguity is a result of his conscious choice not to be tied to his native soil, while he maintains his awareness as a Japanese writer. In fact, in contrast to his avoidance of public, and especially media appearances in Japan, he often expresses himself publicly in speeches, interviews, and award ceremonies abroad by way of fulfilling his responsibility as an internationally recognized Japanese novelist to represent and advocate for his native country.

In chapter 2: "Beyond National Canonicity: Murakami and the Japanese Literary Canon," I address the same issue from the different perspective of a literary canon. Through debating what criteria might canonize a novelist as a Japanese *national* writer, Murakami actually opts out of getting trapped in the canonization process and suggests his intention of going beyond the insular confines.

Murakami considers the writing of novels, especially multivolume ones, central to his identity and social role as a professional writer. On the other hand, he deliberately engages in other kinds of activities between writing novels, such as foreign travels and sports event participations, as well as writing short stories, translations, travel journals, and various essays, lest his mind get exhausted and drained of creativity due to the long, sustained intensity that the making of a novel requires. Thus, all of the seemingly unrelated aspects of his life organically converge on the purpose of fiction writing.

In the biographical sketch above, I included some aspects of Murakami's personal life, such as certain hobbies, precisely because they are closely linked to his act of writing. For instance, according to Murakami, his enthusiasm for music is essential to his writing: when he composes fiction, he pays closest attention to the *rhythm* of a sentence or a passage deriving from musical patterns as he understands them from his vast and intensive exposure to music. And his writings, fictional or otherwise, abound in musical references and thematic allusions. In a similar manner, two of his other activities, running and translating, inseparably correlate to his fiction writing. Thus, in chapter 3: "Translation as a Beneficial Diversion for Murakami's Fiction Writing," I explore the interrelation among these three elements. According to Murakami, in order to write a novel, apart from simply acquiring stamina for months of focused writing, a novelist needs a healthy, well-exercised body to get into, and cope with the dark, dangerous, subconscious realm of their mind. In addition to the physical stimulation and joy that the exercise brings him, there is a psychological motivation for disciplined running.

While Murakami compares long-distance running to writing a novel for months, and short-distance dashes to writing short stories, it can be argued that translation functions for him metaphorically as mid-distance running. Translating a novel by another writer entails certain language difficulties and requires a period of concentration, but it is a far lighter practice than creating one's own novel from scratch; at the same time, one can discover new aspects about the act of writing itself. Thus, the writer may enjoy the very process of translating a book s/he selects, just as mid-distance running, if voluntary and noncompetitive, is not too hard on the body and mind, and can be enjoyable. That seems to constitute a major reason why Murakami has produced so many translations. At any rate, all of his life choices, artistic attitudes, and activities set Murakami apart from many other Japanese writers and account for the *loneliness* of his position among contemporary Japanese artists.

The second part of this monograph investigates three of Murakami's early short stories, including "The Second Bakery Attack" (1985), "*Zō no shōmetsu* 象の消滅 (The Elephant Vanishes)" (1985), and "TV People" (1989). Unlike many of his untranslated short stories that are obviously intended for quick entertainment, I consider these three pieces not only among the best and most complex of his early writing achievements but also essential to understanding where his main concern lies in his fiction writing as a whole, including his novels. As a group, they thematically, yet discreetly converge on interrelated sociopolitical issues, which often does not apply to the other short pieces. Indicative of their significance, each of the three stories is used as an eponymous piece of a collection of short stories. That is the case in Japan with "The Second Bakery Attack" for the book *The Second Bakery Attack* (1986) and "TV People" for *TV People* (1990). Furthermore, the first collection of Murakami's short stories translated into English appeared in 1993 with the title *The Elephant Vanishes*, and the short story, "The Elephant Vanishes," locates itself as its concluding text with the author's apparent approval.

At the first glance, all of the stories appear absurd and nonsensical, if rather amusing. "The Second Bakery Attack" tells us about a young, newly married couple that, struck by unquenchable hunger in the middle of the night, attack a McDonald's for Big Macs. "The Elephant Vanishes" deals with the inexplicable disappearance of an aged elephant from a suburban town. In "TV People," we find shrunken technicians of an almost identical look carrying a TV set into the protagonist's private and office spaces. Typical of Murakami's fictional pieces until the mid-1990s, the protagonists are invariably male narrators around the age of thirty, enjoying urban amenities with office jobs in a metropolis. As expected, their life is filled with consumer goods and Western popular cultural items. The style of their narration is not elaborate and is easy to follow.

For this kind of representation, Murakami's fiction tends to invite criticism of frivolousness and irrelevance. Upon a closer reading, however, such criticism turns out to be misguided, and each of the three stories suggests a serious concern. Albeit amusingly, "The Second Bakery Attack" exposes the capitalist mechanism that incorporates people, even those with dissident aspirations, as its willing subjects. Similarly, "The Elephant Vanishes" reveals how the logic of capitalism disposes of beings, human or otherwise, once it deems them no longer useful. Finally, people get stripped of their autonomy as thinking individuals through media infiltration in "TV People." Fundamentally, the stories have in common Murakami's unwavering antipathy toward sociopolitical power, what he calls the System, directed not at particular individuals or organizations but against a hardly definable and tangible power complex that oppresses humans into total submission. This distrust of power systems originates in his high school days and was probably reinforced during college student demonstrations. Manifest in his independent business entrepreneurship in disregard of an office career as well as in the unusually political statement at Jerusalem, the distrust and resistance to oppressive power structures are already present in these early short stories. They constantly resurface in various forms through novels, especially major ones such as *A Wind-Up Bird Chronicle*, *Kafka on the Shore*, and *1Q84*.

The last chapter, "Televisual Appropriation and Fear in 'TV People' and *Ringu*," is a kind of spin-off, in which I compare "TV People" with a pair of popular Japanese horror movies, *Ringu*. Both came out in the last decade of the twentieth century, with the same image of a nonhuman form coming out of a TV set. Far from a mere coincidence, the similarity suggests the danger people unconsciously feel about deep immersion and entrapment in electronic media.

People take pleasure in reading Murakami's fiction in many languages across the world. And, consigning the understanding of his fiction to each reader, Murakami refuses to not only analyze his own work but also acknowledge and affirm interpretive readings by others. As a result, readers might often encounter a hermetic impasse in understanding the content due to his highly distinctive imagination and apparent lack of meaning. Indeed, his fiction is well known for such difficulty. In face of Murakami's disregard of literary criticism, I hope that this series of essays will provide a bewildered reader with clues to analytically approaching his literary oeuvre as a whole, and literary critics with points for further debate.

NOTE

1. In his recently published journal article, Murakami exceptionally talks about his father's life and his relationship with the parent since his childhood in some detail. See "*Neko wo suteru*" (2019). The article was included in a book with the same main title one year later.

Acknowledgments

I would like to express my gratitude to the following journals for permission to use, in this monograph, articles previously published with them.

Chapter 1, "Murakami's Self-Conscious Ambivalence as a Japanese Writer," was originally published in *The Proceedings of the 5th Annual International Conference on Language, Literature and Linguistics* (L3, 2016) with the title, "Murakami Haruki as an Ambivalently Japanese Writer," and it is published here with a permission from the Global Science and Technology Forum (GSTF) with some modifications.

Chapter 2, "Beyond National Canonicity: Murakami and the Japanese Literary Canon," was originally published in *Southeast Review of Asian Studies* 34 (2012) with the title, "Murakami Haruki's Canon." Chapter 3, "Translation as a Beneficial Diversion for Murakami's Fiction Writing," was originally published in *Southeast Review of Asian Studies* 36 (2014) with the title, "Murakami Haruki the Translator." Both chapters are published here with a permission from *Southeast Review of Asian Studies* with some modifications.

Chapter 4, "'The Second Bakery Attack': The Induced Burial of Young Aspirations," was originally published in *Japan Studies Review* 17 (2013) with the title, "A Bakery Attack Foiled Again." Chapter 5, "'The Elephant Vanishes': What Efficiency Produces," was originally published in *Japan Studies Review* 20 (2016) with the title, "The Creature Disappears for Our Convenience." Chapter 6, "'TV People': The Slick Assault by Electronic Media," was published in *Japan Studies Review* 24 (2020) with the title, "The Infiltrated Self in

Murakami Haruki's 'TV People.'" The three chapters are published here with a permission from *Japan Studies Review* with some modifications.

Chapter 7, "Televisual Appropriation and Fear in 'TV People' and *Ringu*," was originally published in *Philology at MGIMO* 19.3 (2019) with the title, "The Televisually Compromised Spaces in *Ringu* and 'TV People,'" and it is published here with a permission from *Philology at MGIMO* with some modifications.

I am grateful to the editors of all the abovementioned journals/proceedings, especially Dr. Steven Heine and Ms. Maria Sol Echarren at Florida International University who have accepted, processed, and published my articles, including those on Murakami, in *Japan Studies Review* over the last two decades as its editor in chief and an editor, respectively.

I am indebted to Ms. Holly Buchanan as my acquisitions editor at Lexington Books. She kindly accepted my manuscript proposal, responded conscientiously in correspondence for my manuscript preparation, and made the publication of this book possible, all during several months in the difficult pandemic situation.

Last, I appreciate the long-standing friendship and guidance that I have received from a former colleague of mine at the University of Georgia, Dr. Mihai Spariosu. His suggestions regarding book publication always proved to be valuable, including the care he took to ensure the quality of the manuscript of this monograph.

Chapter 1
Murakami's Self-Conscious Ambivalence as a Japanese Writer

In the last few decades, Murakami Haruki has gained a reputation as one of the most popular writers in many parts of the world, including his native land. It is partly because he considers it of paramount importance to connect to his readers anywhere through his stories, as he explains in one of his recent books, *Shokugyō toshite no shōsetsuka* 職業としての小説家 (*The Novelist as an Occupation*) (2015). The book indicates his solid sense of identity now established as a professional literary writer, although he did not intend to be one when he embarked upon his first novel almost accidentally with an epiphany in April 1978. As to how he is perceived in terms of his cultural identity, however, there is a curious, significant discrepancy among his readership. The Japanese readers naturally regard him unquestionably as a Japanese writer who was born and grew up in Japan, has a Japanese name, and whose works they read in the original language.

By contrast, international people outside Japan often find Murakami's fiction basically devoid of native cultural orientation, which renders him a rather non-Japanese novelist for them in spite of their full awareness that he is from Japan. At the same time, a few others, mainly critics and scholars, attempt to figure out his Japanese essence. In this situation, it is meaningful to examine his own words contextually in some of his untranslated nonfictional texts in order to see how the author positions himself culturally as a contemporary writer. This should be of interest to his readers, especially those who do not have either access to his writings in Japanese or an opportunity to approach them in a comprehensive way, to a better understanding of their enigmatic novelist.

His fiction shows a heavily Westernized world filled with mostly American cultural and consumer items, such as music, films, novels, and food, although it is set in Japanese society. Apart from a few proper names of people and places, any mention of what is identifiably Japanese is scarce if any. For instance, his novels until the early 2000s carefully avoid referring to any other Japanese writers. Mishima Yukio 三島由紀夫 (1925–1970) and Ōe Kenzaburō 大江健三郎 (b. 1935) are briefly mentioned at the beginning of *A Wild Sheep Chase*. But the text never refers to Ōe again, and Mishima's case actually demonstrates young people's indifference to the reactionary writer two generations older who staged a failed coup in 1970. Murakami's selective representation of fictionalized Japan obviously reflects his personal preferences. More importantly, the manipulation is likely strategized for today's globalized world of the commercially uniformized market that is cosmopolitan only in a Western sense. As a result, a cultural orientation tied to a specific national/ethnic identity largely loses validity, and it is easy for regular non-Japanese readers to relate to his story through their daily experiences on a personal level rather than being beguiled with exoticism.

Given the divergent perceptions of him, an essential question hinges on how Murakami considers his own cultural identity as a writer. In his untranslated nonfiction, he directly and even unabashedly expresses his personal penchant for Western, especially American culture that began during his adolescence in Kobe. It was very common for his generation of baby boomers, who spent their teenage years in the 1960s, to get willingly immersed in a cultural infusion from the West. Even so, his case is excessive. Indicative of the predilection he has developed, his works, fictional or nonfictional, not only abound in Western references of his choice but also meticulously exclude almost all aspects of the Japanese culture—popular and contemporary as well as traditional—to which he must certainly have been exposed. In this sense, Japan, in his fiction, is heavily biased and reflects no more than a sliver of sociocultural reality.

The author does not deny the skewed nature of his representation, which is apparent in some of his titles, such as *Norwegian Wood*, *Sputnik Sweetheart*, *Kafka on the Shore*, and *What I Talk about When I Talk about Running*. They manifest either his personal likings or his tributes to the Western writers he admires, like Franz Kafka and Raymond Carver in the last two examples. None of his writings are titled similarly after Japanese items or writers.

This stance extends to the language he uses. When he wrote his first novel, *Hear the Wind Sing* (1979), he wanted to forgo the emotion-ridden, aesthetics-infused traditional "system language" of Japanese literature in search of his own writing voice (*"Umibe no Kafuka"* [2003c] 38).[1] For this objective, he first wrote the initial chapter in English and then translated it into Japanese with simple phrasings, relatively short sentences, and a quick reading rhythm (*Shokugyō* [2015] 45–50). The style thus achieved largely characterized Murakami's writings for many years. On a more fundamental level, he detaches himself from a wholehearted embrace of his mother tongue through close self-examination.

According to him, he has treated his native tongue like "a pseudo-foreign language" in order not to be too familiar with it (*"Hon'yaku suru koto"* [1996] 69). He "translates an original text inside [him] into" Japanese, which requires him to "reconstruct the meaning of phrases practically from zero," like translation.[2] He thus maintains a critical distance from the native tongue in which he writes. I will discuss this aspect further in chapter 3 of the present monograph.

Dismissive and even defiant of his native culture as he might appear to be, Murakami's attitude toward it is far from straightforward. For instance, although he proficiently reads English to the extent that translating from modern and contemporary American literature constitutes another major part of his successful writing career, he uses only his native tongue in his own creative writings. Conscious of his status as an established professional writer, he is evidently more attentive to delicate nuances and the expressiveness of the language than when he was young, and he has incorporated conventional literary expressions and longer sentences as he matured as a writer. He remains averse to traditional lyricism and aestheticism, however.

In terms of his relation to Japanese culture, Murakami does state that he is interested in what inerasably remains Japanese in his works despite the unconventional style he employs. It is "a unique kind of pre-modernity" in which reality and unreality coexist side by side and "traversing the border this way or that is natural and smooth, depending on the situation" (*"Umibe no Kafuka"* [2003c] 13–14, 16, 38–39). Uncharacteristically, he cites as an example a classical title, *Ugetsu monogatari* 雨月物語 (*The Tales of Rain and Moon*) (1776) by Ueda Akinari 上田秋成 (1734–1809), which is a collection of ghost stories in the "premodern" Edo Period (*"Umibe no Kafuka"* [2003c] 11–12, 13). He thus ascribes strange occurrences in his fiction to the intrinsically East Asian sensitivity to nature, in which human society and the other world somewhat overlap and easily cross over each other. By contrast, "the two worlds are rather clearly separated from each other" in the West (*"Umibe no Kafuka"* [2003c] 14), as illustrated by the Greek myth of Orpheus in which the archetypal bard fails to bring back his wife Eurydice from the underworld of the dead. Murakami, therefore, infers that this "premodern" worldview is the basis of the widespread acceptance of his novels in such countries as China, Korea, and Taiwan in addition to Japan (*"écrire"* [2003b] 100; *"Afutā Dāku"* [2005c] 189–90; *"Seichō"* [2009d] 51–52; *Shokugyō* [2015] 287). In this respect, for all his abundant incorporation of Western culture, an important basis of his creativity comes from the premodern elements of Japanese/East Asian cultures latent in himself, rather than subscribing to Western concepts like postmodernism, with which literary critics in the West tend to discuss his fiction.

In fact, Murakami tends to reject the postmodern label on his stories (*"Afutā Dāku"* [2005c] 189–90; see also "Art of Fiction" [2004b] 139 and

"*Seichō*" [2009d] 49, 51). As his popularity expanded to other parts of the world outside East Asia, he has identified a large-scale, transnational, sociopolitical reason, beyond "magic realism and postmodernism," why his novels resonate with readers in some regions. For instance, since the 1990s, "a certain kind of chaotic situation" has come into being in Russia and Europe as a result of dismantlement of political and ideological systems, as well as the rise of various forces, such as "fundamentalism ... regionalism ... globalism vs. anti-globalism, mega capitalism and environmentalism." Due to the new situation, people have come to live habitually with a sense of "loss of reality," thereby being rendered more receptive to his novels, and this also applies to the United States to a great extent ("*Seichō*" [2009d] 47–50; see also "*Umibe no Kafuka*" [2003c] 39 and *Shokugyō* [2015] 284–86). Murakami further speculates about its implications for Japan and the rest of East Asia. He suggests that "such a comprehensive landslide" has been "self-evidently, naturally ... felt since an earlier time" as "an ever continuous situation" in the region. East Asia has not even properly undergone "'the modern' that should have occurred prior to 'the postmodern'" (*Shokugyō* [2015] 286–87; see also "*Afutā Dāku*" [2005c] 189–90).

Such an insight into the world situation, derived from his frequent travels, stays abroad, and self-analysis of his writing profession, has enhanced Murakami's awareness as a Japanese writer rather than simply turning him into a cosmopolitan one. In spite of "the neutral style" that he has developed ("*Umibe no Kafuka*" [2003c] 36, 38; *Shokugyō* [2015] 48), he has been "interested from the beginning in how the Japanese live in this world" ("*Umibe no Kafuka*" [2003c] 38). Unlike his well-known aversion to public appearances in Japan, he even considers it "a sort of responsibility ... as one Japanese writer" to expose himself and represent his native culture abroad on such occasions as speech deliveries, public readings, and literary award receptions ("*Seichō*" [2009d] 66–67). He does not fail to note, however, that he is "not particularly patriotic." If he stops being "an expatriate," that metaphorically means a return "not *to his* [native] *soil itself*" but "only to the 'relationship'" with it (*Shokugyō* [2015] 293, the added emphasis in the original text).

Along this line of thought, as I point out in chapter 2, Murakami has little ambition to be enshrined in the canon of Japanese national writers. On the one hand, in response to an inquiry by a Korean reader, he affirms that his writings in Japanese factually amount to no more than a part of "pure Japanese literature." On the other hand, at a more personal, deeper level, his professional philosophy that rejects "the Japanese literary language" overcomes "a kind of impasse into which a lot of 'orthodox' Japanese literature has fallen" (*Koredake* [2006c] 195). In the early 1990s, he speculated on the possibility of "a certain degree of breakthrough" that would vitalize Japanese literature, somewhat comparable to what had happened to Latin American literature, by "relativizing the Japanese language once again while writing novels in Japanese" (*Yagate* [1994] 119). While expressive of his concern for contemporary Japanese literature in general, the idea at the same time points to his aforementioned method of fiction writing as well as to his global perspective. After having explored different styles in his novels, he has expressed his desire to write a lengthy narrative "crucible-like" with diverse characters and perspectives, which he calls *sōgō shōsetsu* 総合小説 "(a comprehensive novel)," in emulation of Dostoevsky's *Demons* (1871–1872) and *The Brothers Karamazov* (1880) ("*Seichō*" [2009d] 53–57; see also "*Umibe no Kafuka*" [2003c] 41). A series of his multivolume novels, including *The Wind-Up Bird Chronicle*, *Kafka on the Shore*, and *1Q84*, likely show his attempts at a comprehensive novel that has never successfully been written in his native land.

To these ends, Murakami adopts materials and social settings from Japan very selectively, with a supranational resonance, and utilizes the Japanese language in an often humorous, relatively simple style that poses few cultural impediments. He basically avoids the literary establishment in Tokyo while refusing to subscribe to the traditional literary language, and he even stays away from his homeland ever so often. That way of life and philosophy does not make him *borderless* or *stateless*, however, when he keeps the full awareness of his position as a Japanese writer who interests his readers, domestic and beyond, with pleasurable stories while delving into vaguely felt, yet unspecified social and psychological layers. The ambivalence inherent in his cultural identity largely comes from choice, which distinguishes him from novelists of older generations and contributes to his standing as a Japanese writer of an international dimension who is neither confined to nor abides by the sociocultural realities of his origin.

NOTES

1. Unless otherwise noted, all the translations from Japanese texts are mine.
2. "*Haruki Murakami: écrire, c'est comme rêver éveillé*" (2003b): 98. All the translations from this French article are mine.

Chapter 2

Beyond National Canonicity
Murakami and the Japanese Literary Canon

In 2006, Jay Rubin published a new English translation of short stories by Akutagawa Ryūnosuke 芥川龍之介 (1892–1927), titled *Rashōmon and Seventeen Other Stories*. Rubin is one of the principal translators of Murakami's works into English as well, and Murakami contributed an introduction with the title, "Akutagawa Ryūnosuke: Downfall of the Chosen."[1] Before commenting on the Akutagawa pieces included in Rubin's book, Murakami ponders on which writers qualify as the ten most important "Japanese national writers" since the Meiji Restoration in 1868, with Akutagawa considered an unquestionable inclusion. Murakami, whom some critics consider a pop writer of inconsequential merit, evidently takes the question of literary canonization seriously. This fact is itself worth noting.

Murakami enumerates three criteria for his exclusive listing. First, a top national writer must have written "works of the first rank that vividly reflect the mentality" of his or her contemporary Japan. Second, his or her "character or life" must have induced "widespread respect or strong sympathy." Third, such a writer must have written works of extensive popular appeal, especially pieces that are "easy enough" for young people to read and memorize, and that may be included "in the nation's primary and middle-school textbooks" (xix–xx). With these criteria in mind, he mentions certain prominent writers of prose fiction from the last 150 years, including Natsume Sōseki 夏目漱石 (1867–1916), Mori Ōgai 森鴎外 (1862–1922), Shimazaki Tōson 島崎藤村 (1872–1943), Shiga Naoya 志賀直哉 (1883–1971), Tanizaki Jun'ichirō 谷崎潤一郎 (1886–1965), and Kawabata Yasunari 川端康成 (1899–1972), in addition to Akutagawa. He mentions two more writers of lesser qualification, Dazai Osamu 太宰治 (1909–1948) and Mishima Yukio (1925–1970), and he concludes that he is unable to decide on "a good candidate for tenth place" (xxxvi).

7

While showing Murakami to be well versed in modern Japanese literature despite his stated disinterest therein, this list roughly coincides with and consciously endorses a common perception of the prose part of the national literature. For instance, he places Natsume atop his list, reflecting the latter's enormous popularity. Although he does not argue for the impartiality of his selections, Murakami apparently aims at it when he candidly admits his personal lack of appreciation for Kawabata and indifference to Shiga and Shimazaki. While he at least recognizes Kawabata's novelistic achievements, he acknowledges that he has not read deeply in Shiga and Shimazaki and that their work has made little impression on him. In spite of this indifference, he includes these three writers in a gesture of fair-mindedness and respect for the cultural consensus.

When closely examined, however, the list raises questions. The first criterion is natural and inevitable, but the second and third are less straightforward, depending on historical and cultural contexts. The second criterion particularly illustrates the problem. Murakami's first seven writers named were influential not only as writers but also as cultural figures far into the second half of the twentieth century. Apart from Natsume, to whom people customarily refer by his penname Sōseki out of a sense of respect and familiarity, however, it is questionable whether these writers were in a position to play a significant public role. Kawabata, Shiga, and Shimazaki, for example, led lives that were largely private. In this respect, Dazai and Mishima, the two authors whom Murakami tentatively mentions, fare better, partly due to the fact that they died more recently, but mainly because of their relatively sensational lives and deaths—the dissolute helplessness of the former and the nationalistic defiance of the latter. As a result, they still enjoy sympathy or respect among certain constituencies.

The third criterion, involving popular appeal especially among the young, poses even more complex problems. As Murakami notes, most of his authors wrote stories for and about young people, such as Mori's *Maihime* 舞姫 The Dancing Girl) (1890) and *Sanshō dayū* 山椒大夫 (Sanshō the Steward) (1915), Natsume's *Bocchan* 坊ちゃん (*Botchan*) (1906), Shiga's "*Kozō no kamisama* 小僧の神様 (Shopboy's God)" (1920), and Kawabata's *Izu no odoriko* 伊豆の踊子 (*The Dancing Girl of Izu*) (1926). As for Akutagawa, certain short stories readily come to mind, such as "*Hana* 鼻 (The Nose)" (1916), "*Imogayu* 芋粥 (Yam Gruel)" (1916), "*Kumo no ito* 蜘蛛の糸 (The Spider's Thread)" (1918), "*Majutsu* 魔術 (The Art of the Occult)" (1919), and "*To Shi-shun* 杜子春 (Tu Tze–chun)" (1920). Murakami mentions all of these Akutagawa pieces as having read them in his own childhood. Dazai's "*Hashire Merosu* 走れメロス (Run, Melos!)" (1940) is widely known, precisely due to the story's inclusion in school textbooks, as stipulated by Murakami's third criterion.

The first problem pertains to changes in textual experience. As Murakami concedes, there are probably not many readers, and most certainly not young ones, who have read through Tanizaki's voluminous representative work *Sasameyuki* 細雪 (*The Makioka Sisters*) (1946–1948). Murakami nevertheless argues that this novel has become accessible to a large audience by virtue of its several cinematic adaptations and has, like the aforementioned stories, thereby "seeped silently into the fertile soil of people's minds to form something like the foundation of the culture or sensibility of the Japanese" (xx). The same issue applies equally to Mishima, for his work is not easily reconciled with popular taste, although a work like *Shiosai* 潮騒 (*The Sound of Waves*) (1954), written in a Greek pastoral mode like *Daphnis and Chloe*, is a possible exception. No matter what "beautiful actresses," or handsome actors for that matter, may feature in filmed versions of these works (xx), however, it is difficult to imagine many of tender age now flocking to theaters to view cinematic adaptations of novels published long before their birth. And new movie renditions of novels by those writers are rare these days. Even if many people have been introduced to the novels in movie theaters or other visual formats, the justification for categorizing movies as a mode of textual experience is tenuous and far-fetched.

Intertwined with the preceding point is another problematic aspect of the third criterion. Murakami's list caters to a somewhat hidebound paradigm. It enumerates nine literary masters of the past, the last of whom died in the early 1970s, while more recent candidates are excluded. Murakami's exclusion of contemporary writers, including himself, is understandable insofar as their reputations have not yet been established and confirmed with the passage of time. But the older writers may already be heading toward relative obscurity. Although the abovementioned pieces by Akutagawa, Dazai, and Natsume may be capable of charming modern audiences, it is doubtful that the general public now has firsthand knowledge of works by the other old masters through direct or even indirect exposure. As discussed above, Mishima and Tanizaki face difficulties in this regard, and Kawabata and Shiga are not likely to fare much better. Shimazaki's early poetry wound its way into the mind of the older generations, but its classical style is probably less palatable and accessible to today's readers. Mori's "Dancing Girl" has the same stylistic impediment, although the story might be tragic and romantic enough to resonate with contemporary readers.

Murakami evidently remains loyal to the literary canon of his younger days, although he supposedly writes from the standpoint of the early twenty-first century. As his discussion indicates, he read a certain range of modern Japanese literature, in spite of personal predilections for Western literature, just as a young person fond of reading in the second half of the twentieth century was expected to. He retains the notions of canonicity prescribed during that era, although his second and third criteria introduce considerations of his own. This reveals a contradiction inherent in his list.

Murakami's third and last criterion is ambiguous as well, for at least two different groups can be placed under the heading of "youth." First, there are elementary and middle school pupils. Second, there are high school and college students. In terms of educational levels, reading skills, and life experience, the two groups must obviously be distinguished. Older students might read stories like *The Dancing Girl of Izu* or novels like *The Makioka Sisters*, despite the generational tendency to eschew printed media. But it is hardly imaginable that the former group, saving a few avid, precocious young readers, has enough will or interest to tackle such works. Those in the younger group are also less likely to view film adaptations of the novels on their own account. At the same time, most of the same younger group are probably familiar with shorter pieces like "The Spider's Web" and "Run, Melos!," thanks in part to the stories' inclusion in school textbooks, and they might be inclined to try longer texts like the humorous *Botchan*.

Equally problematic are certain names that do not appear in Murakami's roster. The issue is threefold. First and fundamentally, one might question how meaningful it is to limit the number of *national* writers to no more than ten. There is the popular tendency to play with *top tens*, but this is hardly an intellectual justification for Murakami's limited purview in the context of the serious discussion at hand.

Second, Murakami's unwillingness or refusal to name a tenth writer must raise eyebrows. Because gender disparity is an obvious aspect of his list, one might be tempted to name a female writer of great merit such as Higuchi Ichiyō 樋口一葉 (1872–1896). Her nomination, however, is problematic due once again to the second and third criteria. The female writer who exceeds all others in the Japanese literary tradition, Murasaki Shikibu 紫式部 (ca. 973–ca. 1014 or 1025), to whom *Genji monogatari* 源氏物語 (*The Tale of Genji*) is ascribed, does not qualify for the same reason, not to mention the fact that she lived some thousand years ago.

Third, Murakami ignores writers who have been active more recently. Foremost among the younger generation are Abe Kōbō 安部公房 (1924–1993) and Ōe Kenzaburō (b. 1935). Abe drew on both existentialism and the Theater of the Absurd and is widely recognized for his originality and creativity. Ōe, who professes a kind of internationalist humanism, received the Nobel Prize for Literature in 1994, becoming the second Japanese writer to win the award, following Kawabata who was honored in 1968. Their literary merits are indisputable. Yet Ōe and Abe do not qualify as "national writers" as Murakami defines the term. Their works, especially Abe's, do not so much "reflect the mentality" of contemporary Japan as point to problems inherent in the supranational social milieu that also colors modern Japan. And it is also hard to argue that the authors' characters or lives have engendered "widespread respect or strong sympathy," especially with Abe. He has largely fallen out of favor from today's reading public. In this respect, Ōe fares better with his own generation and immediately following ones as well as through self-acknowledged commitment to his handicapped son. Above all, Murakami's insistence that canonical literature must speak to Japanese youth tends to scuttle their qualifications for canonicity.

There is at least one writer who meets all the three criteria but is excluded from Murakami's list. That is Miyazawa Kenji 宮澤賢治 (1896–1933), who lived in a remote region of Tohoku. Free of narrow provincialism despite his locale and possessing a deep, essentially humanistic regard for all creatures, his work, which comprises prose and poetry, is highly esteemed in Japan. His sincere spirit of altruism has resonated with succeeding generations, even though readers may not have understood or embraced the religious fervor that underlies his real-life devotion. This high regard is exemplified with a specific poem of thirty lines, usually called "*Ame nimo makezu* 雨ニモマケズ (Not Succumbing to the Rain)" in keeping with its first line. Written in the simple *katakana* 片仮名 script, the poem expresses an unassuming, yet earnest wish for a selfless way of life. This short poem has maintained a strong hold on the Japanese psyche. Following the seismic, tsunami, and nuclear disasters that literally and metaphorically shook the foundation of the Japanese nation in March 2011, the poem featured in many public ceremonies, indicating its *national* character.

Miyazawa's poetry widely varies in style (conventional, experimental), diction (standard, dialectal, religious, scientific), and religious, philosophical depth, while most of his prose pieces take the form of children's tales that nevertheless contain a profound message more attuned to mature understanding. Japanese readers tend to be very familiar with some of these works, having been exposed to them since childhood in school textbooks and other media. In sum, Miyazawa easily clears the difficult hurdles of Murakami's second and third criteria of the list in question. The absence of Miyazawa's name therefrom is apparently due to the Tokyo-centric view of national literature that the list clearly evinces and Murakami shares in spite of his origin in western Japan. If Murakami disqualifies Miyazawa simply because of the form of his stories for children, including the imaginatively large-scale, very popular *Gingatesudō no yoru* 銀河鉄道の夜 (*A Night on the Galaxy Railroad*), that would contradict not only his third criterion for young readers but also his regard for children's stories. Murakami has translated several of them from English to Japanese in the absence of his own.

Murakami is more akin to the other two writers he omits, Abe and Ōe, than to those listed. Similar to their cases, especially Abe's, in reading any of his novels or short stories, one immediately notices a shortage or even lack of reference to his native culture. Instead, his fiction immerses itself in certain fields of Western cultural knowledge, disregarding most aspects of the Japanese cultural reality, both high/traditional and popular/contemporary. In his fiction, Japan functions as little more than a hypothesized locale for a story that might be set anywhere in today's world of highly capitalized urbanity. In this sense, his work obviously fails to meet fully his own first criterion: that national literature should "vividly reflect the mentality" of contemporary Japan. Although pointing to the part of contemporary Japanese society, the flamboyant globalism of Murakami's work disqualifies him as a national writer in his own definition.

Furthermore, Murakami's fairly consistent antipathy to media exposure, which is manifest in his self-effacing, fairly reclusive lifestyle, defies his second criterion. The case, however, is not without a certain complexity. Much of his nonfiction provides us with glimpses of his opinions and private life, such as his preferences for certain kinds of music and his enthusiasm for running. And he is more inclined to speak publicly while abroad and to grant interviews to Western publications. Furthermore, he has responded to his readers' questions via a temporary website. In spite of his well-known aversion to media and publicity, then, he desires to touch others in various forms and to be unobtrusively understood as an individual and as a writer.

The third criterion likewise requires complex evaluation with regard to the age of readership. There is no question that much of Murakami's work has a strong popular appeal. Murakami does not primarily write for school-age children, but many of his writings abound in humor likely to appeal to a teenage audience. While they may be baffled by Murakami's unconventional representation, younger readers can enjoy the strengths of his storytelling, and they may even unwittingly absorb some of his masked meaning. In addition, some high school textbooks have begun to include his pieces, and it remains to be seen how that form of publication lastingly helps them to "seep silently into the fertile soil of" young people's minds on a national, collective level.

The ultimate question is how to conceive Murakami in the light of his own three criteria of canonicity. As discussed above, his first criterion that typifies the logic of national canon formation qualifies him only partially. His second and third criteria set more difficult hurdles for his inclusion. This suggests that Murakami has no particular ambition to be enshrined in the canon of Japanese national writers, and his professional aspirations transcend the limitations of a national boundary. To this global end, he works on not too specifically Japanese subject matters and sociocultural settings for a widespread resonance and writes in a humorous, relatively simple style that presents few cultural impediments. On this basis, we should consider Murakami's canonical considerations only marginally relevant to himself. They reveal a conception of national literature that his own work does not adopt.

NOTE

1. "Akutagawa" (2006a). All the references in this chapter are to this introduction.

Chapter 3

Translation as a Beneficial Diversion for Murakami's Fiction Writing

Outside of his native land, Murakami Haruki is widely recognized as the most accessible Japanese writer with his works translated into many languages. They include several long novels, a number of mid-sized novels, and short stories. Indicative of his prolificity as it is, this list actually proves partial, for his writing is far from limited to fiction. His oeuvre also includes numerous pieces of translation and nonfiction, including essays, travel journals, and interviews. Out of these two categories, the latter is at least known to English-speaking countries with the translation of *What I Talk about When I Talk about Running* along with a few other essays. By contrast, it is not well known in the West that he has translated a considerable amount of literary fiction, mainly by American writers, into Japanese. It is important to point out the significance that Murakami's translation carries in his overall activities as a professional writer.

The list of his translations from modern and contemporary American literature is quite extensive and diverse, including works by C. D. B. Bryan (1936–2009), Truman Capote (1924–1984), Raymond Carver (1938–1988), Raymond Chandler (1888–1959), F. Scott Fitzgerald (1896–1940), Mikal Gilmore (b. 1951), Mark Helprin (b. 1947), John Irving (b. 1942), Ursula K. Le Guin (1929–2018), William Timothy-O'Brien (b. 1946), Grace Paley (1922–2007), J. D. Salinger (1919–2010), Shel Silverstein (1930–1999), Mark Strand (1934–2014), Paul Theroux (b. 1941), Chris Van Allsburg (b. 1949), and several others to date.

There are a number of reasons for Murakami's fascination with American literature. He belongs to the first post–World War II generation that grew up under heavy influences from American culture. Three of the favorite novels from his teenage years are Salinger's *Catcher in the Rye*, Chandler's *Long Goodbye*, and Fitzgerald's *Great Gatsby*, all of which he eventually translated into Japanese, despite widely accepted versions previously made by other translators. Since the 1980s, he has visited the United States on many occasions, including extended stays with visiting scholarships at Princeton University and Tufts University in the early 1990s, enabling him to make direct contact with some of the contemporary American writers whom he highly regards. They include, for instance, O'Brien and Paley when they gave speeches at Princeton and in New York City, respectively. At Princeton, he made good friends with Mary Morris (b. 1947), while he admits having felt somewhat awed at English Department luncheons in the presence of dignitaries like Toni Morrison (1931–2019) and Joyce Carol Oates (b. 1938) ("Art of Fiction" [2004b] 124). In 1984, he took an early morning jog in Central Park with Irving, who suggested it in lieu of a regular interview (*Hashiru koto* [2007a] 239). In the same year, Murakami also visited Raymond Carver at his home on the Olympic Peninsula in Washington State. Murakami is an ardent admirer of Carver and has translated his complete works into Japanese.[1] Such personal contact was obviously impossible with Fitzgerald, but thanks to his translation of Fitzgerald's novels and his own novels translated into English, Murakami was invited over a weekend to the home of the American writer's granddaughter in a small village near Philadelphia during his Princeton days (*Yagate* [1994] 50–63).

Apart from the fact that he highly esteems these American writers, there are several reasons for his considerable commitment to translation. On the practical side, although his great reverence for Kafka and Dostoevsky, for instance, is well documented, he does not have enough linguistic proficiency in any other foreign languages than English to venture a commercially viable and professionally refined translation. By contrast, he is fluent in English, especially for reading. The first book he read in English is *The Name Is Archer* (1955) by Ross Macdonald (Kenneth Millar) (1915–1983), a copy of which he picked up as a high school student at a used bookstore frequented by international visitors to the port city of Kobe ("Art of Fiction" [2004b] 125). Thereafter, almost an inborn rebel against the social system of Japan, he developed his personal habit of reading fiction in English outside of English classes at school (*Hon'yaku yawa* [2000] 56). As a result, he has full capability of appreciating English texts in the original, albeit on his own terms, and that personal reading skill has eventually evolved into a passion for translation.

Other reasons for his commitment to translation are more directly linked to his writing profession. He is very conscious of his works translated into many languages, not only because of his authorship but also because he himself is a translator who knows all the challenges of this undertaking. It is one of his pleasures during trips abroad to find his translated books on bookstore shelves ("*Hon'yaku no kamisama*" [2008] 5). Since he does not read foreign language books with confidence except in English, he initially did not pay much attention to the accuracy of his books translated into other languages, simply feeling gratitude for the translators and answering their questions. Even when he was asked to check English versions, he gave minimal suggestions to the translators, while enjoying reading them as if they were new stories to him, because he generally does not reread his works, once published, in Japanese. The reading experience of his translated work thus allows him to reexamine it objectively (*"Hon'yaku suru koto"* [1996] 68–69; *Hon'yaku yawa* [2000] 19–20, 28–29, 77). By the early 2000s, however, he realized that, due to scarcity of professionals who can translate directly from Japanese, the English versions, not the originals, are sometimes translated into other languages. Since then, he has come to believe that close attention should be paid to the accuracy of English translations (*Hon'yaku yawa* [2000] 82–83; "Art of Fiction" [2004b] 138).

Even more significantly, Murakami's practice as a translator converges with his writing profession in three ways. First, he considers translating rather like a personal pleasure (*"Hon'yaku no kamisama"* [2008] 4). This does not mean that he makes light of translation. He simply enjoys the very act of translation that brings about "an unsurpassed, intangible bounty," even though that process likely requires patient commitment to overcome certain difficulties (*Hon'yaku yawa* [2000] 4, 50, 80–81, 110; the English word "bounty" used in the original). He "let[s] each line of his] favorite works pass through [his] body and [his] mind" ("Art of Fiction" [2004b] 125). By contrast, once he embarks on writing a novel, he maintains a rigorous, self-imposed schedule by forcing himself to sit at the desk for a set number of hours every day, for months, whether he can actually write with inspiration or not. He calls this writing regimen "the Chandler method," after Raymond Chandler whose advice about how to write a novel he remembers having read (*asahi-dō haihō* [1989] 42–46). Needless to say, the entire task of constructing a novel from scratch in this way is mentally exhaustive.

At the same time, he explains that his fiction writing essentially undergoes the same process as translating, for he has consistently dealt with his native tongue like "a pseudo-foreign language," in order to avoid too close familiarity with it (*"Hon'yaku suru koto"* [1996] 69). He translates "the original text inside [him]" into Japanese (*"écrire"* [2003b] 98). This suggests that he first conceives his story as a non-Japanese proto-text in his fiction-making, only to dismantle it so that it can by necessity be reconstructed "from zero" as a readable Japanese text. Accordingly, his fiction writing is "a formative operation entirely separate" from fiction-making (*"écrire"* [2003b] 98). In this sense, his "creative writing and translating . . . might rather be two sides of the same coin" (*"Hon'yaku suru koto"* [1996] 69). Therefore, he is used to the act of translation on a fundamental level through fiction writing ("*écrire*" [2003b] 98), further enabling him to take pleasure in actual translation.

Second, Murakami professionally benefits from translating pieces by other writers (*Hon'yaku yawa 2* [2003a] 7). Because he treats Japanese like a foreign language and does not consider the highly aestheticized style of earlier writers (like Mishima and Kawabata) compatible with his own, he rebels against the national literary tradition and seeks to learn from foreign writers ("*écrire*" [2003b] 98; "*Umibe no Kafuka*" [2003c] 38). He accesses their novels in the original, later translating many of them into Japanese (*Hon'yaku yawa* [2000] 219–20). Because "translation is an extremely dense reading" (*Hon'yaku yawa* [2000] 199), translating from English enables him to understand the merit of a certain style more clearly than is possible through mere reading (*Hon'yaku yawa* [2000] 57–59, 110–12; "*Hon'yaku no kamisama*" [2008] 4–5). It is very similar to the practice of "copying" or "trac[ing] the writing in good books" through which people could learn many aspects of writing in the past (*Hon'yaku yawa* [2000] 57–58; "Look Here's America" [2006b] 153). He even personifies the act of translation as "at once an important teacher of style and a good literary friend" whom he has constantly trusted ("*Hon'yaku no kamisama*" [2008] 5; see also "*écrire*" [2003b] 98).

Understandably, he chooses to translate "books from which [he] could learn something" ("Art of Fiction" [2004b] 138; see also *Hon'yaku yawa* [2000] 40, 87–88, 200, 237–38). For instance, he claims to have learned a "powerful storytelling voice" from Irving, because what he gains through translation is not practical technicalities but "a big thing," such as "the author's breathing, his perspective, his sensations" ("Look Here's America" [2006b] 153). Contrary to the Western reader's expectation, he avoids translating postmodern works by such writers as John Barth, Don DeLillo, and Thomas Pynchon, to whom he is often compared, for he anticipates "a crash—[his] insanity against their insanity." Instead, the writers he rather chooses for translation are "realistic writers," because "[t]heir work requires a very close reading to translate" ("Art of Fiction" [2004b] 139). At the same time, he prefers writers like Carver and O'Brien, whose works occasionally become "irrational," on the ground that he somehow feels "more comfortable when things are messy" ("Look Here's America" [2006b] 153).

Third, he intentionally alternates between different kinds of writing. As with translation, he basically writes short stories for personal pleasure. Although he can finish a short story within a week, he "often completes a set of five or six short stories intensively in one to two months," because that manner of composition renders them correlative and meaningful to each other.[2] Importantly, he does not write a novel while he is writing a group of short stories, thereby providing himself with a period of respite from the intensity of writing a single fictional narrative of considerable length.

Similarly, but with a much shorter or irregular cycle, Murakami utilizes translation to enhance his capacity for producing novels. He "translates when [he] is not writing a novel and writes a novel when [he] wants to" ("*Seichō*" [2009d] 72; see also *Hon'yaku yawa* [2000] 37–38, 208; "*Hon'yaku no kamisama*" [2008] 4). For instance, he "spent several months writing a long novel in the mornings and recovering from the fatigue by translating (Chandler's *Farewell, My Lovely* [1940]) in the afternoons" ("*Herajika*" [2009b] 34). He purposefully avoids writing novels exclusively one after another, interspersing long periods of writing with diversions like foreign travel and athletic competition. More significantly, for creativity's sake, he chooses to write short stories and nonfictional pieces or make translations. This is essential in order to relieve himself not only of mental exhaustion but also of the dangers of psychological disequilibrium that can come out of writing novels about the fear and violence inherent in today's society ("In Dreams Begins" [2005d] 558–59; see also *Hon'yaku yawa* [2000] 16, 198–99; "*écrire*" [2003b] 99–100; "*Seichō*" [2009d] 10).

Murakami often compares writing to another of his passions, running. In a discussion of the difference between writing a novel and writing short stories, he metaphorically explains:

> I am originally a long-distance runner. To run a long distance, however, I not only need to gain stamina but also develop inner muscles [with sprints] systematically. My belief is that a work of profundity only becomes possible with an effective combination of [muscular] explosiveness and durability. ("*Jūgo no shitsumon*" [2007b] 37)

If writing a novel is analogous to running a marathon and creating short stories to short-distance dashes, a relevant question here is what translating would compare to. Although Murakami does not provide an answer, it must be a relatively short- or mid-distance running that is not intended as a competitive race or a serious preparation for it. Translation would rather approximate a self-controlled, yet joyous run to make occasionally with a respected friend, like the jog he took with John Irving one morning in 1984. He might not be able to articulate much of his own thought while running, but he learns greatly, even philosophically, by steadily observing how his running mate manages the exercise. And that practice strengthens his will and ability to run his course at different levels, making various kinds of running and writing possible in years to come. It follows that translation plays a vital, integral role in maintaining his prolific career as a writer of fiction.

Now that we have laid the foundation for our understanding of his writing activities, we will begin to discuss specific texts individually in the next three chapters. They are the three short stories that I consider important in

Murakami's early writing career for the reasons I specified in foreword. In addition to illustrating the points I have been making so far, the argument will help to demonstrate where his main concerns reside.

NOTES

1. "*Reimondo Kāvā*" (2004a) 228, 230. Murakami's homage to Carver is also apparent in the title of his collected essays about running, *What I Talk about When I Talk about Running*, modeled after Carver's collection of short stories, *What We Talk about When We Talk about Love*, with the approval of Carver's widow Tess Gallagher. See *Hashiru koto* (2007a) 241.

2. "*jūgo no shitsumon*" (2007b) 37; "*Seichō*" (2009d) 43–44. *Men without Women* (2014) is an example of this method of composition. He originally published five of the collection's six short stories in magazines over a few months from 2013 to 2014. The sixth story was written specifically for the collection. They share a motif that the title suggests.

Chapter 4

"The Second Bakery Attack"
The Induced Burial of Young Aspirations

"*Pan'ya saishūgeki* パン屋再襲撃 (The Second Bakery Attack)" first came out in 1985 and was included one year later in a book format with six of Murakami's other mid-1980s short stories. Placed at the very beginning as the book's title piece, this particular story occupies a prominent position in the collection, although a married couple's assault for food commodities in the middle of the night makes little sense at first and appears merely entertaining for a quick read. According to Fukami Haruka, "what makes this work interesting" as "a mere game" comes from "the bizarre originality to seek an absolute basis upon what is totally wild, unfounded, and incompatible with economic efficiency" (Fukami 159–60). By contrast, Kawai Toshio argues that "beneath its apparently superficial pop style," Murakami's fiction tends to reveal "a certain depth of general consciousness" (Kawai 193). Far from being nonsensical, the story in question indicates the author's concern for a generational transformation with a combination of postindustrial generalities and historical particularities. The representation is at once magically realistic of the contemporary predicament and psychoanalytically illustrative of the unconscious condition.

THE SOCIOPOLITICAL DIMENSION

As might be expected, a story about the supposedly identical narrator's prior *attack* exists with the title, "*Pan'ya shūgeki*パン屋襲撃 (The Bakery Attack)" (1981), which provides details as well as discrepancies with the later text about the first incident. For instance, some humorous, yet apparently unessential elements, such as a middle-aged woman of excessively careful deliberation on purchase of a few pieces of bread and a pair of impractically gigantic nail clippers on the store counter, are deleted in the later story. Given its brevity and obvious jokes, the early story does not invite much serious consideration, but the use of certain idioms, such as "lack of equivalent exchange items" that causes the two college-age attackers' hunger and the "thesis" and "ideology" that the observing narrator attributes to the woman's careful, yet tardy selection process, nevertheless suggests a significant textual substratum.[1] The most revealing is the baker's identity as a communist party member who enthuses over Wagner's opera. This contradictory identity does confuse the narrator, and the author omits the party affiliation in the second story, not only to reduce the degree of joking license and confusion but also probably to diffuse apparent political implications.

Like many other college students of his generation, Murakami participated in demonstrations against the 1970 renewal of the U.S.-Japan Security Treaty as potentially driving the nation into U.S.-led military conflicts in the Cold War, with Vietnam as an ongoing, imminent example. The student movement in the late 1960s ideologically veered toward the left in reaction to the conservative government, although it functioned largely independent of any direct party control. This political distancing explains the mocking, discrediting portrayal of the bald baker in his fifties as an unlikely, ineffectual communist who, content with his small business, admiringly listens to Wagner in tedium. The efforts to block the security treaty renewal led to the students' anarchist tendencies to subvert order and authorities, such as their universities, if not ambitiously ushering in an outright revolution as yet. This anarchist stance is manifest, for instance, when, declaring that "God, Marx, John Lennon are all dead," the narrator and his friend, probably roommates and destitute, decide to "take to evildoing" of an intended assault and, if necessary, even murders in the first story (*"PS"* 31). Reminiscing in the second story, the narrator claims that they were "attackers, not robbers," who by choice refused to work for a wage as socially conditioned and "did some pretty awful things to get [their] hands on food,"[2] thereby professing their antisocial, noncapitalistic activism as distinct from plain sloth.

Apart from humor and the narrator's musical preference that juxtaposes a former Beatles member with pivots of major belief systems in spiritualism and materialism, this passing reference points to an authorial intention in his remaking of the old story, for a temporal discrepancy exists between the two texts. The reference to Lennon's death in December of 1980 and the publication of *"Pan'ya shūgeki"* in October of 1981 locate the first story at the beginning of the 1980s.[3] In "The Second Bakery Attack," published in 1985, the narrator reflects on the original attack as having taken place some ten years earlier, which dates the incident in the middle of the 1970s or earlier.[4] Since the second story basically follows what happens in the first, this time difference is probably attributable to two factors. First, Murakami had no plan to make a sequel when he wrote the first story. Second, by design, he necessarily set the attack of the second story no later than its publication date so that the reminisced original attack could coincide with the period when the effects of the student movement were at least still felt, although irreversibly waning, and Japan was yet to attain the apex of its unprecedented economic prosperity in the 1980s. This temporal manipulation also attests to the possibility of a serious reading.

In fact, critics have associated this and some of Murakami's other fictions with the sociopolitical situation of his young days.[5] In "The Second Bakery Attack," the wife dictates a modification of their target from a genuine bakery (which they cannot by any means find open anywhere in the city after 2:30 a.m.) to a McDonald's, calling the fast-food restaurant "something like a bakery" in expedient justification for her self-admitted compromise.[6] Then, she takes all the initiatives. Using a self-adhesive tape, she promptly covers the car number plates with "a practiced efficiency to her movements" ("SBA" 45), equips herself and her inept husband with such essential items as ski masks and an automatic shotgun for the attack at hand, and tells him to act as she instructs. He does not understand at all why she possesses those objects, only feeling that "married life is weird" ("SBA" 44).

Weird as it is, Katō Norihiro links this aspect of the story to the 1971–1972 incidents by a small group of extreme leftists, called *Rengō sekigun* 連合赤軍 (the United Red Army), who got radicalized as remnants of the failed student movements against the security treaty renewal.[7] After having attacked a gun store to obtain firearms and ammunitions, they concealed themselves in a mountainous region of central Japan for a year, lynching their own members and, when detected and besieged, confronting the advancing police with fatal shooting. Murakami has maintained strong interest in this incident, as most notably demonstrated by one of his major novels, *1Q84*, in which a group of people seclude themselves in the same inland region for their ideological pursuit as a result of their failed student protest around 1970.[8]

It would be amiss, however, to interpret a text solely with a perspective that specifically focuses on particular social circumstances within certain national boundaries at a given historical moment. Such a reading would not account for the ardent popularity Murakami's translated oeuvre enjoys in many parts of the world. The reader outside his native land, or even in it for that matter, would likely appreciate "The Second Bakery Attack" without any prior knowledge of the leftist movements, including the United Red Army incidents that happened in Japan several decades ago. For the same reason, Matthew Carl Strecher's argument that Murakami's works gained popularity due to their introduction to the world market in the 1980s when Japan's emergence "as a modern world superpower" was drawing international attention has proven only partially valid (Strecher 6), for the popularity has not only endured but also considerably expanded ever since the burst of the bubble economy at the beginning of the 1990s.

Rather than delving into historical particularities, let us assume that the story's appeal lies in its general nature. For instance, it would probably not be a rare experience for a young couple married for just a few weeks to find out, while adjusting to the constant presence of another and barely establishing "a mutual understanding" of life together ("*PSS*" 12), an unexpected aspect of which the new partner did not have the slightest inkling before in the spouse's way of life. That might not be deft familiarity with ski masks, a shotgun, and other necessities for attacking a business establishment, but much less agitative, more ordinary objects or matters would be sufficient to astonish an unsuspecting partner and make him/her consider "married life weird." Instead of the mundane, however, Murakami typically utilizes a technique akin to Kafkaesque representation and magical realism, thereby elucidating a certain problem inherent in people's lives that they might vaguely sense, but not necessarily be conscious of. In the current case, the sudden appearance of a shotgun and so on can be regarded as indicative of his regular writing mode rather than as referring to a particular actual incident.

If a part of the story can be understood in this way, the whole text can likewise assume general significance not tied to a specific past occurrence. In a word, "The Second Bakery Attack," along with its earlier version, is not so much a mere aftermath episode of unsuccessful student revolt as a coming-of-age tale in which the youth is unwittingly, yet irretrievably incorporated into the social machinery. In "*Pan'ya shūgeki*," after the bored baker finds his willingness to let the would-be assailants eat for free rejected, he casually proposes to curse them, because, according to the narrator, "there must be some exchange" ("*PS*" 35), the idea that brings in a basis of social contract in their dealing. As the attackers hate to be cursed and the baker does not wish to be killed, the two young men immediately agree to his next suggestion that they become fond of Wagner in exchange for free bread, which means to listen to *Tristan and Isolde* while eating on-site. With both sides satisfied, the deal seems fair and innocuous, and the curse does not appear to take effect.

A fairly curious, random choice as it might appear to be, Wagner's music occupies a culturally central position in this Japanese story, as the staple food indispensable enough to be obtained by force for survival is not rice in any forms but store-baked bread. Likely strategized for today's commercially uniformized world market, Murakami's fictions reflect his personal preferences. Especially in his early ones, his stories are characteristically almost devoid of references, a few proper names set aside, to any forms of his native culture, replaced by an abundance of Western counterparts. As a result, cultural orientation tied to specific national/ethnic identity loses validity. In this context, Wagner's opera at the bakery symbolizes canonized music and, as such, the established social order or discourse.⁹ The narrator aptly calls the baker's maneuvering "Wagner propaganda" ("SBA" 41).¹⁰ Acquiescing to accept the composition signifies to be part of the system, unknowingly succumbing oneself to its yoke at the expense of a young aspiration to be rebellious and independent. At the same time, the German composer's grandiose romanticization of ancient mythology and medievalism devalues and trivializes ordinary life in modernity by implied contrast, thereby enhancing haunting subordination through implicit valorization.

Lulling and obscuring the hunger, which probably stands for unfulfilled, persistent, yet indefinable ambition of youth, the curse of social imposition sets in and stays potently internalized like, in the wife's words, "a toothache that will torment [him] until his death unless destroyed by [his] own hands" ("*PSS*" 20). Suggestively, although the two men declare no interest in Wagner's music and, only prompted by the deal, profess to like it for the moment's convenience, the narrator later remembers the precise titles of the pieces they heard on that occasion. In this context, the giant nail clippers on the bakery counter, which the narrator regards as some kind of joke in the early story, symbolize apparatuses. These include staple food distribution and culturally encoded music for depriving people, especially youth, of their innately subversive antipathy to the state and social control in which both communism and capitalism take part hand in hand here. A glance at the seemingly impractical tool *clips* the two men's initial elation for carrying out a violent attack (see Kazamaru 60). It is as if, "defanged and declawed by the baker, the two men were turned into domesticated 'social animals'" (Ishikura 197). As a result, in exchange for the disappearance of the hunger's "nihility," the narrator feels his self-autonomous capacity of "imagination" for decisive action irreversibly compromised "like rolling down a gentle slope with a clatter" thanks to unforced coercion of society at the end of "*Pan'ya shūgeki*" ("*PS*" 36).

Thus, ten years later in "The Second Bakery Attack," recalling the forgotten memory, and occasioned by the resurgent hunger, the narrator tells his wife that the two hunger-driven men agreed to the deal with the baker, divested now of communist affiliation, because listening to an LP record of Wagner opera preludes, including those to *Tannhaüser* and *The Flying Dutchman*, is "not labor in the pure sense of the word" and is therefore acceptable. But they felt later "some grave mistake" lurking in the "business-like transaction" that cast a "dark shadow on [their] lives . . . undoubtedly as a kind of curse" ("*PSS*" 17, 19). Since then, his life, like that of others of his age, has gradually undergone many expected changes, such as graduation, regular employment, and meeting a future spouse.

In tandem with his generation's conservative ethos change for order and stability, he has now become settled in marriage and no longer averse to working, out of all occupational possibilities, at a law firm while preparing for the bar exam. The old partner's whereabouts have been unknown since the two men parted company after their diverted attack, although it can easily be surmised that he has taken a similar course of life. At present, the curse affects both the narrator, now self-admittedly socially docile and complicit, and his new partner, as which the wife defines herself.

In a sense, their case is relatively fortunate. In some of Murakami's other stories, such as *A Wild Sheep Chase*, "TV People," and *The Wind-Up Bird Chronicle*, similarly married couples as young white-collar professionals, aged alike, living childless in an urban apartment, and busy to maintain their fledging middle-class status, barely find sufficient time to meet and talk to each other. Although married for some years, they, or at least the narrating husbands, lack meaningful communication and understanding, causing their wives to disappear from their lives without their knowing how that has come to pass. They fail to notice, in their moral slumber, a grave problem latent in the daily routines to which they have congenially got accustomed in the course of their marital life.

In the present case, the couple's problem is of somewhat different nature precisely due to the early stage of their conjugality. As Ishikura Michiko points out, the scant provisions in the refrigerator, which the narrator ascribes to their busy work schedules, symbolize their incomplete status as a married couple (Ishikura 191). Kept awake by painful hunger late at night, this fresh pair of wife and husband can set themselves to deal with a common, pressing situation in the form of hunger and a curse, which originate in a spouse's past. More experienced couples would customarily try, albeit in vain, to go back to sleep for the early start of their jobs the following day. Their bakery attack translates into their first serious attempt to lay a foundation for "a mutual understanding" in their two weeks of married life during which she has constantly sensed "existence of a certain kind of curse close by" ("*PSS*" 20). In this sense, the question that the wife raises at the beginning, whether the hunger "has anything to do with being married" ("SBA" 39), is highly relevant.

We should note that the curse and the hunger are not one and the same.[11] Although the wife's attack declaration originates in shared hunger and from her desire to get rid of the curse, she never directly identifies one with the other. After having compared the curse to a toothache for its likely future effect combined with the hunger's pain, she refines her simile, based on how she personally feels, to a "heavy, dusty curtain that hasn't been washed for years, hanging down from the ceiling" on her mind during their short, married life ("SBA" 43). Her phrasing indicates a kind of indefinable mental gloom that sharply contrasts to the hunger's keen, physical sensation. The hunger is linked to the core of intrinsic search for one's *raison d'être*, while the curse that begins with eating bread offered through a compromise is associated with the expediency of accommodating oneself to extrinsic circumstances. Like the curtain, the curse has covered with a sense of material fulfillment the hunger that has remained potential in an inner part of the mind for a decade. When the new partnership of marriage divides the curse between wife and husband, its potency gets temporarily diluted, and the suppressed hunger resurfaces with relentlessly intense vengeance. Her proposal of a reenacted attack means to address the root causes of the problem at once by responding properly to youthful, unquenched ardor and regaining mental autonomy as individuals from social exploitation.

To dispel the curse, the married couple in their late twenties *plunder* a McDonald's. To maintain their anarchist legitimacy, the narrator refrains from devouring freshly made Big Macs in the restaurant despite a pressing hunger, while his wife pays for two large cups of Coke because they only have to acquire bread by force and nothing else for the task's completion. After the wife binds the three employees skillfully and caringly with a packing cord she has brought, they successfully drive away with thirty takeout Big Macs plus the Coke, and they can finally assuage the unbearable hunger with one-third of the hamburgers at a parking lot. The story appears to have a resolution to their problem.

The question remains, however, whether "the curse is cleared away" (Kobayashi 119), although starvation has dissipated. First of all, a McDonald's is a far cry from a genuine bakery. On the most basic level, the franchised store does not bake bread on its premises. The effect of the attack at such a gross compromise is highly questionable. Second, similar to the baker, the three employees at the McDonald's offer no resistance. Instead, the manager meekly insists to give away more money than worth thirty Big Macs to purchase at another store, or even all the night's earnings that are insured, for simplifying the day's accounting in favor of what the store manual dictates. The system is thus considered even more important than life at risk. While the attackers do not yield to a tempting offer this time, the effect they desire becomes likely attenuated and unattainable when the meaning of the attack intended as a terrorizing, subversive act is evidently misplaced and lost. After all, the action they carry out for the removal of a curse amounts to "no more than a mere attack for attack's sake" (Matsui 168), a mere shell of assault that does not involve any other compelling need or ideology. The wife herself dismantles the significance of their *attack* when she pays for their soft drinks as a good citizen.

Third, the McDonald's globally promotes its presence and products with utmost efficiency and American cultural orientation. Considering the political circumstances of this story in which the leftist student revolt was directed against Japan's military alliance with the United States, the couple's compromised solution poses a contradiction. But they wholeheartedly savor the smell and taste of ten Big Macs, six for him and four for her. Although frequent references to globally marketed, mainly Western, and especially American consumer products and cultural items, such as John Lennon in the early text and *The Wizard of Oz* in the later one, commonly feature in Murakami's works, the unquestioned, willing consumption of so many Big Macs proves problematic to their intended solution.

In fact, certain signs indicate failure in the couple's endeavor to eradicate the curse. Apart from the two attackers and the three employees, only two more people are present as customers in the midnight restaurant. They are a student-looking couple that, fast asleep on the plastic table with two cups of strawberry milkshake, never wake up during the attack, even when the shutter comes down with a roar at the wife's order. While the narrator wonders at their unusually deep sleep, these two minor figures that have come out for a late-night meal on a red, shiny, sporty car parked outside are probably representative, as Katō argues (Katō 227–28), of the younger generation that unconditionally accepts the sociopolitical reality and enjoys the material prosperity of Japan in the 1980s and thereafter. This is one of the two original generational groups that the main readership of Murakami's literature in Japan consists of.

Born around 1960 or later, growing up during a rapid economic expansion, they tend to be ideologically apolitical and noncommittal while primarily knowing how to express self-identity through what and how much they consume, like the couple's choice of a late-night snack and a new mid-sized automobile that costs more with an alluring promotional image than the attackers' secondhand, compact, practical model.[12] A shared taste for fast food notwithstanding, this young couple's case makes a sharp contrast to the attackers', in the sense that one cup of McDonald's milkshake alone is apparently enough not only to quench their physical and mental *thirst*, if any, but also to keep them in deep, undisturbed sleep, whereas he and his wife cannot sleep due to the critically severe *hunger*, although they have eaten the previous evening. In this context, we can easily infer that McDonald's food items affect the younger couple as an institutional sedative, just as the baker's bread has succeeded in keeping the narrator's initially challenging spirit stifled and buried. Immersed in the system from childhood, the younger generation does not even remotely suspect or feel the social manipulation as a kind of curse.

Another short story by Murakami, titled *"Nemuri* 眠り (Sleep)" (1989), is relevant here as synthetic of the two couples' cases. The narrating female protagonist, who conventionally regards herself as happily married with a child, is metaphorically sound *asleep* under the spell of social norms. Once she entertains a doubt about the meaning of her married life, however, she never regains a wink of sleep for weeks with her critical awakening. It is noteworthy, then, that one major effect of the hunger in "The Second

Bakery Attack" is to keep the married couple awake from falling back to sleep or the regularity of their everyday life that obscures and blocks self-questioning.

The other group of potential readers is Murakami's college-educated postwar generation. With certain sympathy, they can find the projection of their politically frustrated youth in some of his stories, and their skeptical view of the following generation is reflected through the narrator in the author's satirical gaze at the young couple who are undisturbedly asleep. Their case, however, is hardly dissimilar in terms of the metamorphosis that they have undergone since college graduation. They at once constituted the driving force of the 1980s economic prosperity and were greatly receptive of its material benefits albeit once critical of the status quo, and now faintly reminiscent of the resistant stance they formerly assumed. This is what the narrator means by gradual, irreversible changes that have befallen him.[13]

Thus, when the attackers consume ten Big Macs to their heart's content, they not only fill their physical need but also, with twenty more hamburgers to go, replace a remnant of youthful drive for change with unbridled consumerism. The void in the form of hunger is simply overridden with what the largest multinational franchise system offers. With the curse not lifted but further internally solidified, the couple are fully incorporated into the established system of predominantly economic efficacy despite their last rebellious undertaking. As Fredric Jameson speculates concerning the colonizing power of "multinational capital" on the unconscious, "local countercultural forms of cultural resistance and guerilla warfare . . . are all somehow secretly disarmed and reabsorbed by a system of which they themselves might well be considered a part, since they can achieve no distance from it" (Jameson 49). Without "solid . . . subjectivity" to "confront reality" and distinguish themselves from others anymore, they have become "beings that can be deciphered in any way as signs" like the commodities they consume (Tanaka 190–91; see also Morimoto 92; Matsui 162–63, 166–68, 169).

The attackers and the college-aged customers each exhibit a fantastically opposite extremity of physical symptom, that is, sudden unfathomable hunger that keeps one awake and undisturbedly deep sleep. In spite of an apparent, generational difference, however, these symptoms actually indicate their fundamental affinity and high involvement with socioeconomic reality. In Kobayashi Masaaki's words, the young diners are "nothing other than negative doubles" of the married pair of attackers and "prototypically can be traced back to" the original attackers who do not resist accepting free bread in their transaction (Kobayashi 121). As if to seal off the reemergent attackers' fate as newly converted devotees of globalized consumerism and the American lifestyle, "a giant SONY BETA ad tower" glows in front of their car at dawn while they listen to Far East Network (FEN), which is a U.S.

military radio station based in western Tokyo, "playing cowboy music" at the end of the story ("SBA" 48).

"The Second Bakery Attack" contains political bearings upon specific historical circumstances, and by extension, it can apply to a certain generation that revolted against establishments at the end of the 1960s in many parts of the world. Murakami states in relation to the nuclear aftermath of March 11, 2011: "What I wanted to say is what I've been saying since 1968: we have to change the system" (Anderson 63). At the same time, the story can be considered more general and far-reaching as allegorical of the final transition of life's stages from youth, which is long gone with an indefinite sense of incompletion, into sedateness of the initially undesired, yet inevitably compromised middle age, anywhere but especially in rapidly capitalized societies. This is, in fact, a major theme in Murakami's early works, to which, together with the dominance of global consumerism and Americanization, any readers can relate, although they might not be aware of detailed historic-political subtleties on the textual surface and beneath.

THE RELATIONAL DIMENSION

The sociopolitical elements discussed above relate to the story's more private aspect of a mutual relationship between two main characters, the narrator and his wife. Apart from the extraordinary hunger they cope with, they at first look very normal as a young, married couple. Living in a metropolitan area, and owning a used Toyota Corolla, they have a middle-class lifestyle that befits young professionals in the early stage of their careers and marriage. Their power dynamics are not balanced, however. Similar to Murakami's other male narrator-protagonists in his early stories, this narrator is not committed in a significant way to any relationships with other people, including the wife and the partner of his younger days in whose life's progress he shows little interest after they severed their tie. Recalling the second bakery attack incident at an unspecified time of his narration,[14] he confides his utter inability to specify in what year he got married and how old he was then, although he can tell the age difference between him and his wife, which remains constant, without any difficulty.

In contrast to his half-hearted commitment to life, which is already evident in his compromising negotiation with the baker in the early story, his wife is much more decisive in thought and action, and she takes the initiative. When struck by the unfathomable hunger, she not only ignores her husband's poor joke about cooking deodorant but also immediately rejects his proposal to look for an all-night restaurant, convincingly asserting that it is wrong to eat out after midnight. When, reminded of a similar experience of starvation a decade ago, he inadvertently mentions his earlier attempt at a bakery assault, she insists on hearing every detail with a number of persistent questions, to which he reluctantly yields. It is she who firmly believes in the sheer necessity of another bakery attack and actually carries it out with expert finesse, while the husband awkwardly follows her directions.

The lack of relational equilibrium between them typically manifests itself in the philosophical way he understands his response to her demand or rejection with the concept of a thesis. The term is a carryover from the earlier story in which, according to the narrator's observation, different kinds of bread compete to occupy "the position of a thesis," meaning a hypothesis or a proposition, in the middle-aged female customer's mind (*"PS"* 32). In "The Second Bakery Attack," as the husband easily concedes to his wife's refusal to go out for a midnight supper, he considers her attitude very old-fashioned, yet he calls her resolute opinion "a thesis (or a statement)" that has to be accepted "like a kind of revelation" (*"PSS"* 14, 13). He ascribes his own readiness to comply with her ideas to a tendency supposedly common among those newly married, which hints at fear to offend a new spouse. But the use of *thesis* twice in this context sets his case apart from other marriages. While ideologically tinged here with its rampant usage by leftist student activists of his generation for their political manifesto, the term *thesis* dialectically presupposes an antithesis or his individual thought that should confront hers, but it is simply absent. Consequently, there is no dialectic synthesis of the two individual elements. Within the present context at least, the relationship turns out to be odd in the sense that it is exclusively one-sided, with no conflict or mutual compromise involved.

As the narrating voice provides both a textual perspective and inner private deliberations, however, the narrator maintains his individual presence throughout the story. Thus, his narration makes the wife's unchallenged assertiveness all the more outstanding, while the unnamed spouse remains not quite developed as a full-fledged character with internal depth. Her characterization consists of narrow facets of externally observed traits, including old-fashioned belief against going out at night, questioning insistence, fastidiousness over paying what she regards as due, decisiveness in words and behavior, and perhaps little capacity for humor. Other than her intuitive idea that they must attack a bakery that very night, she does not express much of her own thought. With the author's magically realistic mode of writing aside, her thorough preparation and skills for burglary, which she has obviously acquired with experience, remain unlikely and enigmatic. Meanwhile, her consistently feminine mode of speech in Japanese, unlike rather neutralized or *unisex* speech among today's generations, is conventionally generic enough to indicate the gender rather than an individual. So is the description of her bodily motion as feline at the end.[15] Although she is one of the only two principal figures in the story, her characterization is largely flat.[16]

This suggests that she functions not only as an independent character to keep the story from falling into solipsism but also, on a symbolic level, as an extension of the narrator's psyche that collaborates with the hunger for compelling the unwilling husband to finalize the unfinished business of attacking a bakery. A strong urge comes from within in the form of hunger, while the wife externally takes all the steps for him to carry out the intended action.[17] As demonstrative of the implicit collaboration, the imagery of a floating boat over a submarine volcano, to which he compares his hunger-stricken situation, is spontaneously introduced to his mind upon his agreeing to her *thesis* of the impropriety to go out for dinner late at night ("SBA" 38). In turn, the image enhances his notion of her statement as an unchallengeable thesis, because his instant acceptance of her admittedly outdated social propriety comes from his intuitive understanding of the induced imagery as "of a revelatory kind" (*"PSS"* 14). His acquiescence to follow her lead is thus closely related to his surging insecurity that stems from a cause far more deep-seated than a mere apprehension for passing offenses.

With regard to insecurity tied to the hunger, Ishikura rather finds it in the wife, arguing that the female character is motivated by her jealousy of the two attackers' partnership in the first bakery assault and her desire to feel unity with her husband. It is not very likely, however, for a wife to feel such jealousy about her husband's past comradery with a friend whom he has not brought to his mind for years. Regardless of the unspecified gender of the *aibō* 相棒 (partner), with which the reminiscing husband refers to his former friend, if the hunger symbolizes intense jealousy and a need for strong relationship in her case (Ishikura 189–91), the same argument ill applies to the hunger of the original two accomplices in the first attack as well as to that of her husband. In *"Pan'ya shūgeki,"* the narrator refers to his *partner* with masculine pronouns in accordance with the common usage of the word that is unlikely to indicate a female partner, especially in a love relationship. Accordingly, the wife's abrupt self-proclamation as such in marriage rather indicates her urgent sense of need to act like a figuratively male accomplice for a successful robbery that would hopefully result in a better marital relationship with her husband.

The association of the wife with the underwater volcano in terms of his rising insecurity is ascertainable through the rest of the story with four more references to the volcano. The second reference introduces the other metaphor of "a hermetically sealed cavern" ("SBA" 39) around the stomach, and both metaphors center on the strong sense of uncertainty linked to the unfathomable hunger. In fact, the two metaphors emerge immediately after she expresses her dismay at the excessive hunger that plagues her and asks the husband if the condition is somehow related to the state of being married. Although he does not know the answer and replies so, her question not only prompts the cavernous image in his mind but also reminds him of a similar hunger that he once had ten years ago, unintentionally mentioning a long-forgotten bakery attack for the first time and thereby causing her persistent inquiries. As she intensifies her questioning and insists on the necessity to undertake another bakery attack, waves caused by submarine earthquakes rock the narrator's imaginary boat in the third and fourth references, while the seawater under it becomes threateningly even clearer than before, highly enhancing his sense of uncertainty. Finally, upon the married couple's success in attacking a McDonald's and filling their stomach with plundered Big Macs in a parking lot at dawn, the narrator realizes that the volcano has disappeared. Only ripples lap the boat on the calm sea in his metaphorical world while the satisfied wife gently sleeps on his shoulder in reality.

Evidently, this does not mean that all is well with the couple at the end. Earlier in the story, when she asks him about the outcome of the first bakery attack, he chooses not to tell her much of what actually happened as a result, only saying that his situation has taken many gradual turns, ultimately leading to his current ordinary, unobtrusive life of a job and marriage. Similarly, although we know from the sociopolitical analysis that their efforts to dispel the curse for good with the second attack probably have not produced the expected effect, Murakami avoids delivering the crucial information to the reader. His reticence suggests a mixed result at best. Apparently, we have to delve into a deeper level of textual reading in order to explore the unspoken.

THE PSYCHOLOGICAL DIMENSION

The two aspects discussed so far, sociopolitical and relational, strongly point to a psychological layer that underlies them. In order to describe his abrupt starvation, the narrator uses two similes turned into extended metaphors. One is "a hermetically sealed cavern" around the stomach that gives him a "weird sense . . . of the existential reality of non-existence," causing him an acrophobically "paralyzing fear." The utter void at the center of the body is by nature psychologically problematic. It is nihilistically challenging to the host, bringing about the impending sense of fear, anxiety, and uncertainty that "you might feel when you climb to the very top of a high steeple" ("SBA" 39). The description suggests the severe hunger's origin not exactly from a physical, nutritional need but, more profoundly, from a mental source that might invalidate the life he has lived if not properly and urgently addressed. At the same time, a tightly closed vacuity indicates difficulty in solving the problem.

Chapter 4

The other metaphor of an underwater volcano and a boat that appears five times through the text reinforces the acrophobic state of mind. In explaining the special nature of his hunger, the narrator imagines a volcano top threateningly visible under a small boat from which his vicarious self looks down through the seawater. As the hunger intensifies, the water becomes increasingly so transparent that he can clearly see every detail of the crater at the bottom and feels as if his boat were floating unsupported in the air, thereby rendering the marine situation into an acrophobic impasse. This volcanic metaphor leads to the cavernous one, and both images convey the sensation of tense, precarious unsteadiness. The metaphorical focus differs, however, between sheer vacuity at the physical center of the body and danger waiting deep below to erupt and take over the attentive consciousness above on the surface. Although cited to elucidate the enormity of hunger, the volcanic metaphor actually points, not to the hunger's physically felt oppressiveness but specifically to its purely psychological aspect with the submarine volcano standing for a part of the visualized unconscious, in a text that abounds in similes of "imagery of the deep sea" (Ishikura 200).

This unconsciousness is a contested one. For instance, Kobayashi considers it "a congealed scar of libido repressed in the id field," whereas Ishikura thinks that the volcano stands for the husband's fear of his wife's drive for conjugal unity (Kobayashi 120; Ishikura 201–2). The very first passage about the volcano makes it clear that the underlying issue is psychological, of which the narrator has little doubt when he states that, not being Sigmund Freud, he cannot interpret the image he himself has spontaneously created. He thus divulges a belief, shared by the general public, that the Austrian scholar is the authority in psychoanalysis, and that one should rely on his theory in dealing with the unconscious. The directly visible underwater volcano, however, does not qualify well as the Freudian subconscious in some crucial elements. Freud hypothesizes a stratum under the consciousness, which remains invisibly chaotic, vastly unfathomable, and resists any manipulative intervention by reason, rather affecting the mind significantly in such a covert, distorted, symbolic way as to produce symptoms of repressed desires.

At the same time, the narrator's anonymity suggests that the symbolism possibly applies beyond an individual mold. Murakami often talks about "our generation" in many of his numerous nonfictional writings, meaning the baby boomers who were born shortly after World War II, reached their adolescence in the sixties, and participated in anti-war, anti-establishment student movements toward the decade's end in Japan and elsewhere. His literature as a whole reveals a persistent interest in the various changes, including social, cultural, economic, and political, that his generation has undergone. As discussed earlier, "The Second Bakery Attack" also contains a sociopolitical implication peculiar to the generation as well as a more general significance. What the text signifies can thus extend to a generational, or even supranational, sphere of unconsciousness shared by people of a certain age group regardless of ethnicity. In this respect, it alludes to the Jungian theory as well. Like the Freudian model, however, the outstanding volcano fits ill the vast substratum of the mind that the Swiss psychologist proposes as the collective unconscious. Apart from Murakami's statement not to have subscribed to the Jungian psychoanalysis ("In Dreams Begins" [2005d] 560–61; see also "Author Interviews" [1997b]; *"Umibe no Kafuka"* [2003c] 22), the theory does not suppose an archetype of a massive, immobile, psychic projection rising from the murky nether stratum toward the attentive consciousness.

The unconscious in this story is thus distinctive in a few respects. First, the volcano bottom remains vast and hidden from view while its top is clearly visible from the ocean surface. Second, the large crater protrudes threateningly toward the watchful self that is puny and sensitively vulnerable by contrast. Third, the surface mind can by no means figure out what might lie underneath the highly visible crater or if an eruption will ever occur. The consciousness understands the existence of a vast, lower counterpart without any means to control it. In other words, the narrator is constantly aware of the volcano's massive presence under him with the bird's view-like advantage, but without freedom to flee from it.[18] What actually unsettles him in anticipation, however, is not exactly a sudden outburst of lava and flying rocks at the boat, that is, destruction of the conscious self by unleashed power of the subconscious, which might or might not occur. Rather, it is the increasing water transparency that renders him more and more fearfully aware of what lies below, as if the mountain understood the very nature of impact it gives upon the closely watching self. This almost willful underwater landmass that intimidates the surface consciousness with its own independent presence and subterranean system metaphorically approximates the Lacanian unconscious that *"is structured like a language"* (Lacan 20; italics in the original).

As a spontaneous image that the narrator-protagonist presents to describe his unusual hunger, the volcano belongs to the Imaginary order that Jacques Lacan posits. The image does not stand by itself, however, because it involves language to build an extended metaphor. Although imaginary, the volcano solely depends on the mediation of the words he utilizes. Thus, it also belongs to the Symbolic order as a signifier. In addition, the volcano centers around what cannot be identified, only hinting in the form of a metaphoric image at what can be sensed as real but cannot be referenced through signification. Similar to the cavernous metaphor, it suggests the oxymoronic nonexistence of existence in the midst of being. It follows that the volcanic metaphor locates itself at the intersection of Lacan's three orders: the Imaginary, the Symbolic, and the Real.

The question hinges on what the hunger is symptomatic of as a psychic condition. As demonstrated before, a central issue is rather broadly sociopolitical than sexual in this case. An eruptive volcano suggests danger, violence, and overthrow of the status quo. As such, it can function well as a metaphor for a revolution, which students in the late 1960s aspired to bring about with their protestations, or that which the narrator-protagonist and his friend tried to achieve on a small scale with their intended terrorization at a bakery. But, as the disappointed students were soon incorporated into the social fabric as its core productive members with the lure of economic fulfillment, the two characters accepted the baker's free bread in exchange for their assent to listen to Wagner's preludes. Thus, a dormant volcano deep under the sea suits well as a symbol for a thwarted, revolutionary aspiration.

In the light of Lacanian psychoanalysis, what diverts the rebellious youth into social inertia is the big Other that controls logic, language, and meaning in the Symbolic order. In the present socialized context, the Other stays in full, yet covert play through the baker's conciliatory offer and Wagner's canonical music that succeed in lulling the aspiration. This leaves the subject lacking in an object against which to carry out social subversion, causing him an unfulfilled desire, which has remained latent for ten years due to the internalized curse or the Symbolic intervention. Repressed and structured in the unconscious, however, the desire ultimately reasserts itself as a keenly painful hunger on the physical level and in the imagined form of cavernous and volcanic metaphors.

As a construct of the Imaginary order contained in the Symbolic, this volcano operates on the unseen geological system underneath, which itself constitutes a metaphor for the system of language that structures the Lacanian unconscious. As such, it understands the linguistic workings of the surface mind, but it rejects any conscious attempts to modify it. Thus, the almost willful volcano keeps a possibly imminent eruption beyond the narrator's comprehension. As a result, he remains suspended in high uncertainty, which leads to the imagery of acrophobic impasse. But it does not threaten him with actual volcanic activities. Instead, his growing anxiety in the face of an internal demon or a neglected desire is translated visually into an absence in the form of the increasing water transparency that appears to annul the distance between consciousness and the fermenting unconscious.

The volcano with the potentiality of an eruption is a symptom of the narrator's repressed desire for social change, not a simple "image of nihilism" based on playful, arbitrary meaninglessness as Fukami argues (Fukami 157). Not allowed to find a vent for a decade, the desire turns negatively inverted as lack or want that reemerges as intense hunger in the end. In place of being visualized as a symbolically distorted dream, two metaphors are elaborately crafted with words to manifest it. The nihilistic cavern directly points to the negative enormity of physical want, and the increasing water transparency indicative of the closing gap with the unconscious unsettles the consciousness that remains incapable of understanding its lower counterpart. Meanwhile, the socially imposed curse of the Symbolic order for signification keeps the eruption in check by muffling the desire and forcibly channeling it into the unseen subterranean realm of the Real while allowing it partially and metaphorically visible as an underwater congealed volcano top in the Imaginary order.

The volcanic imagery spontaneously comes to the narrator during conversation with his wife about the hunger that afflicts them both. More precisely, the word *eizō* 映像, which he uses to organize the image into four successive stages at the present time of his narration, actually means an electronic image, more likely a cinematic one. Harking back to Murakami's strong interest in film since youth as mentioned in foreword, the use of this word suggests the narrator's direct or indirect involvement in the image production, whether as a creator or as a spectator. Still, he fails to acknowledge or understand his repressed desire in preference for his current immersion in social compromise, complacency, and sedentariness, although the acknowledged desire might perhaps help to release him from an unresolved problem of his past.

Unfamiliarity with psychoanalysis is his excuse, when, in fact, he lacks the will or courage to "go down to the dark places, to the deep places" unlike the author who "endure[s]" descent into a nightmarish realm of fiction-making ("In Dreams Begins" [2005d] 558–59; see also *"écrire"* [2003b] 99–100; *Hashiru koto* [2007a] 133–37; *Shokugyō* [2015] 175–76). Instead, a rather intuitive, yet unprofessional diagnosis for action quickly comes from his wife. Following her initiative, he participates in a bakery attack as a hesitant, unwilling accomplice, not convinced of its necessity to the very end. As a result, what the two metaphors combined bring about is neither an eruptive outburst of destructive mental energy nor the pent-up desire conducted toward a therapeutic effect but the selfsame energy dissipated and finally substituted with socially sanctioned desires of mature sedateness and unabashed consumerism. Accordingly, the underwater volcano as a symptom disappears from the narrator's observant sight in the end.

"The Second Bakery Attack" is one of the short stories that Murakami Haruki wrote early in his writing career. Easy to read, these stories tend to delineate a strange, absurd, or even impossible occurrence, set in an otherwise ordinary reality, to the reader's amusement or bewilderment. As the author claims to search for a "deeper story within those easy words" of his fiction ("In Dreams Begins" [2005d] 553), it is highly assumable that they contain serious aspects that defy humor-fraught nonchalance on the surface at multiple levels, such as sociopolitical, relational, and psychological. That is to say, some, if not all of those stories with their brevity can rival his much discussed, increasingly voluminous novels in the complex nexus of potential meaning. This particular text stands a close examination and demonstrates that possibility well. To demonstrate this point as well as Murakami's crucial interest further, we shall explore another instance of his early short stories in the next chapter.

NOTES

1. *"Pan'ya shūgeki* パン屋襲撃 (A Bakery Attack)," in *Murakami Haruki zen sakuhin 1979–1989 8: Tanpenshū III* (1991) 31–36. All the references to this text are to this edition, and all the translations from it are mine. The piece is abbreviated as *"PS"* hereafter.

2. "The Second Bakery Attack," trans. Jay Rubin, in *The Elephant Vanishes* (1993) 39. The short story in translation is abbreviated as "SBA," and all the references to the piece noted "SBA" are to this translation.

3. Initially published in the October issue of *Waseda bungaku* that year as *"Pan'ya shūgeki,"* this short story appeared one month later with a different title, *"Pan* (Bread)," in Murakami and Itoi, *Yume de aimashō* (1981).

4. Matsui (160) admits that it is more appropriate to regard the later story as "a work with the eighties' contemporaneity centering on 1985" than, if calculated from the supposed date of the first attack around 1980, as "a kind of future" piece set around 1990.

5. See, for instance, Tanaka 194; Morimoto 90–94; Kazamaru 61–62; Matsui 156–71.

6. *"Pan'ya saishūgeki* パン屋再襲撃 (The Second Bakery Attack)," in *Murakami Haruki zen sakuhin 1979–1989 8* (1991) 23. Unless noted "SBA" as Rubin's translation, all the translations from this original text are mine. The piece in the original is abbreviated as *"PSS"* hereafter.

7. Katō 228–30. Katō asserts that Murakami got the title, "The Second Bakery Attack," from the expression, "the gun shop attack," freshly used in the evening newspapers on the day of the group's action. The news reports ten of the robbed guns as "SKB Remington 5-chambered automatic shotguns (12-caliber)" and "ski caps" left in their abandoned car that had its license number plates disguised.

8. *Ichi-kyū-hachi-yon: bukku wan* (1Q84: Book 1) (2009a) 220–31.

9. It is noteworthy that the prelude to *Tristan and Isolde* accompanies the climax of the film, *Yūkoku* 憂国 (Patriotism) (1966), which Mishima Yukio scripted, produced, directed, and played the principal role of, based on his short story of the same title about double suicide of an army lieutenant and his wife, set against the backdrop of the 2.26 coup d'état attempt in 1936. Apart from resorting to the Wagnerian exuberant lyricism that renders the gruesome scene *Romantic*, Mishima evokes Wagner's canonical authority to endorse the double suicide as a form of dedication to the cause of national integrity.

10. Kobayashi identifies the story's bread with "the bread that the devil showed in the Gospels" and "the bread that 'the Great Inquisitor' of Ivan Karamazov detailed."

He goes as far as to call the propaganda in question "promotion of fascism ideology" (Kobayashi 122). I consider the symbolism of this bread more generally inherent in capitalistic society than rife with specific religious and political allusions.

11. Critics has not pointed out this crucial difference. For instance, although Yoshikawa (15), among others, correctly explains the hunger as a result of the curse, he identifies "the resurgence of what was once familiar but has disappeared" with the curse.

12. In the original text, the sleeping couple's car is specified as a Nissan model called Bluebird that was popular in the 1980s. For more details about this model, see Matsui 166.

13. The change largely applies to Murakami's private life as well in terms of accumulation of possessions, such as CDs and LP records, and a lifestyle that involves cars as well as international trips and stays. This is obvious in many of his nonfictional pieces, and we can also trace the same change in protagonists' modes of life in his fictions.

14. As Tanaka (189) points out, "The Second Bakery Attack" consists of "three layers of time," including the first phase of the initial bakery attack, the second of the narrator's two-week-long marriage leading to the reenacted bakery attack, and the third layer of his narration in retrospect of those past events.

15. We can find another example of this simile in "*UFO ga Kushiro ni oriru* UFOが釧路に降りる (UFO in Kushiro)" (1999).

16. This might be partly because, "in Murakami's works, women in reality tend to exist as the unintelligible others" in contrast to "women in virtual worlds as objects of adoration" as Ishikura (194) argues. According to Matsui (165), using similes for caricature, the narrator in this story views his wife as "different from him."

17. With regard to female characters in his fiction, Murakami states in a 2004 interview ("Art of Fiction" [2004b] 133): "Women are mediums, in a sense: the function of the medium is to make something happen through her. . . . The protagonist is always led somewhere by the medium, and the visions that he sees are shown to him by her." See also "Sean Wilsey" (2005b) 247.

18. According to Ragland-Sullivan (75), Lacan compares the human consciousness to "a boat cut loose from its moorings," because, "detached from any direct access to its own unconscious knowledge, the human subject is also adrift."

Chapter 5

"The Elephant Vanishes"
What Efficiency Produces

The Elephant Vanishes came out in 1993 as the first English collection of short stories by Murakami Haruki. Selecting from existing Japanese pieces, it was "another new collection reedited" that "an American publisher originally made" (Aoyama 252, 238). Among them, "The Second Bakery Attack" (1985) and "TV People" (1989) mark the early stage of the author's writing career in the sense that they were title pieces of Japanese collections, respectively, in 1986 and 1990. But they do not receive special arrangement in the English version with seventeen pieces. By contrast, although originally positioned second after the title piece at the beginning of the Japanese book *Pan'ya saishūgeki* パン屋再襲撃 (*The Second Bakery Attack*) (1986), the short story "Zō no shōmetsu 象の消滅 (The Elephant Vanishes)" (1985) assumes dual significance in the English translated edition as its eponymous text and with its placement at the very end. This added significance might partly come from a marketing consideration with the perplexingly appealing title.[1] Still, the story has not attracted much critical attention, presumably considered frivolous on account of the reader's difficulty in making sense, or even "an ultimate negation to convey a story with some actual meaning attached to it other than the story itself."[2]

My assumption here is that the physical effacement of an elephant in the text is indeed not supposed to allow a rational explanation and is expected to remain a mystery. This does not mean, however, that the reading experience of "The Elephant Vanishes" yields little interpretative understanding. As Wada Atsuhiko points out, an unspecified, yet central issue is economic efficiency, and, despite his skepticism, it is certainly possible to figure out to a great extent, for instance, the root cause of the protagonist's "tendency to get attracted to what the elephant stands for" as well as "the gap that lies between" the two main characters (Wada 163). In addition, what makes this text outstanding is not the Kafkaesque weirdness of the story told but the fact that the text as a whole is structurally unstable, with a discrepancy between imaginatively unusual content and sharply divided form. It is not "a comforting text" about irretrievable loss that "finds a way how to get along with the system rather than criticize it" (Wada 160). A persistent sense of antipathy to the socioeconomic system underlies apparent irrationality of the essentially disquieting text, aimed at "the problematic and incompletely conceptualized relationships between the individual and society" in postindustrial reality (Kawakami 310).

As often the case with Murakami's early fictional pieces, an unnamed man around the age of thirty, more specifically thirty-one years old by the end of September in this case, narrates the story about an unrealistic, even absurd occurrence. Unmarried, he lives alone in an unspecified *town*, commuting to a company as an office worker. As a suburban municipality near a metropolis like Tokyo, his *town* is large enough to have an increasing number of high-rise, expensive apartment buildings and urban facilities, such as a small-scale zoo, although the zoo has been closed due to financial difficulties. The story concerns, as the title literally indicates, the sudden disappearance of a very aged elephant, so old that no other zoos care to take it. The animal's physical existence, along with its old keeper, simply and mysteriously vanishes without leaving any trace from within a small enclosure allotted for it, reportedly sometime between early evening on May 17 and the following afternoon. Having paid attention to the animal since the zoo's closure, the narrator closely follows TV and magazine coverage of the aftermath and exclusively collects all the newspaper articles about the incident in scrapbooks. The public interest, however, dwindles in a week, and a few more months are enough to erase the memory from people's minds, except for his.

This account takes up the work's first half. Uncharacteristic of Murakami's regular writing, this section reveals social satire clearly targeted at hypocrisy and hardly disguised greed of the expanding city. The narrator's perusal of available information and his direct observation of certain events expose the town's budget-conscious partisan politics, entrepreneurship that pursues profits at minimal costs, and the media sensationalism that seeks to agitate the easily swayable public opinion with news frenzy. Although the narrator does not directly comment on them, he apparently does not approve of these social reactions, judging from the way he observes them in a detached, yet somewhat ridiculing way.

Otherwise, this portion of the story exhibits the Japanese writer's typical style and imagination à la Franz Kafka, particularly reminiscent of *The Metamorphosis* (1915) in terms of central nonhuman creatures. The Czech writer pioneered the textual reconfiguration of reality through presenting a grotesquely unreal situation in minute detail almost to the point of precluding disbelief and incredibility. It is a well-known fact that Murakami pays devout homage to Kafka, to the extent that one of his major novels is titled *Kafka on the Shore* with the namesake teenage protagonist. In addition, highly shy of media exposure and publicity as he is, Murakami nevertheless chose to receive in person the 2006 Kafka Prize in Prague, citing for the exceptional public appearance his great admiration of the Czech predecessor. As a result, Kafka's influence on Murakami's writing is manifest on a technical level, exemplified in the current case by the real-life-like news reporting surrounding the giant animal's mysterious disappearance. More importantly, Kafka's fiction hints at a problem in society, which is too insidiously pervasive for people to recognize it. In order to bring the underlying issue to the forefront of the reader's awareness, the fiction shockingly destroys expectation of literary protocols and life's continuum with frightening imagination actualized in uncompromisingly daily normalcy, and this applies to Murakami's fiction as well.

There are at least three differences, however. First, compared with Gregor Samsa's sudden transformation into a large insect, for instance, the disappearance of an elephant might appear innocuous, even humorous. This is not to deny Kafka's sense of humor, but many of Murakami's oeuvres tend to exhibit relatively lighthearted humor unlike Kafka's, which is often dark and abstruse. Second, what relates Murakami's fictional world to today's life is not only close attention to detail but also abundant references to consumer goods and popular items predominantly of Western culture, which saturate his characters' lives in their daily routines. Third, in a different way from Kafka's fiction in which an individual faces an inexorable, incomprehensible system that rigidly constitutes the social fabric, Murakami's character one day finds him/herself somehow placed in an almost identical, yet somewhat altered reality. The nature of reality alters itself without any dramatically telltale signs, while the protagonist initially undergoes no internal or external transformation. In this regard, Murkakami's novel *1Q84* offers a typical example. In turn, the short story at hand somehow throws the protagonist into a partially warped reality of a shrinking elephant.

These three points are conducive to some critics' denouncement of Murakami's fiction as frivolous and irrelevant to grave social issues.[3] Still, in terms of foregrounding an unrecognized condition latent in familiar reality through effects of shock and humor, he follows in Kafka's steps. The question, then, is what Murakami seeks to expose and make people realize from behind the façade of frivolity and inexplicable unreality in the midst of normalcy. It is neither the social milieu that demands unconditional devotion at the sacrifice of individual self-integrity as in *The Metamorphosis* nor the highly organized, rigid system of legal régime or bureaucratic authority that seeks its own end, regardless of citizens' rights or interests as in *The Trial*

(1925) and *The Castle* (1926). Murakami hints at an even more indescribable or unspecific situation inherent in the very regular way we live our contemporary life that causes us unacknowledged anxiety.

The key lies in what truly differentiates this story. It is neither the absurdity of the elephant's putative escape nor, as the narrator eventually reveals, unreality of its gradual shrinkage. Murakami's fiction abounds in the sudden, inexplicable disappearance of characters,[4] and a shrunken size of beings is also used in such works as "TV People" and *1Q84*. What makes "The Elephant Vanishes" unusual and distinctive among his works is its composition that consists of equally divided, yet ill-connected halves. In the original Japanese publication of the book *Pan'ya saishūgeki*, the first section of "The Elephant Vanishes" has fourteen pages (35–48), followed by the second section of another fourteen pages (49–62), with the dividing middle coinciding with the folding between p. 48 and p. 49.[5] In the English translation,[6] the division between the two sections is patently marked with a blank line on p. 318, and it also occurs in the middle of the story if a half empty space of its first page is taken into consideration.[7]

As we have seen, the first section reveals the narrator carefully and persistently following the newspaper articles and TV reports that do not and cannot yield any conclusive evidence or statement about the missing elephant. The second part begins after a hiatus of a few months toward the end of September, when we find the narrator at a business party as an able public relations worker for a major electronic appliance company, advertising a new set of coordinated kitchen products to women's magazines. He meets an editor, a woman five years younger, from one of those magazines. Both being single, young professionals in the prime of their lives, they find each other attractive and continue their dialogue at a cocktail bar after the party. In these somewhat informal circumstances, he inadvertently confides in her about his recent secret. Prompted by her, he reluctantly claims to have been the last witness of the animal and its keeper from a distance, hesitantly asserting that the elephant was physically shrinking before the lights were turned off in the house to close the view.

With the same number of pages, the two sections do not interrelate to each other in a meaningful way, except for the same narrator and the account of an improbable impossibility. The first section mainly consists of the protagonist's narration, and the second section of a dialogue between him and the editor. This might be construed as a narratological experimentation by the author who has tried various forms of fiction in terms of modes (realistic, imaginary, and mixed), voices (first- and third-person narrations), and length (short, mid-sized, and long) during his writing career. Murakami also experimented with alternate chapters, in which two unrelated plots unfold in parallel only to converge toward the end, in two of his major novels,

Hard-Boiled Wonderland and the End of the World and *1Q84*. The current case differs from this narrative technique, however. It also diverges from an ending that does not connect well with the preceding main body as in *South of the Border, West of the Sun* and *The Sputnik Sweetheart*. In these mid-sized novels, the male narrator-protagonist drags on with his daily routine without a resolution after a leading female character mysteriously disappears.

It is the sharp disaccord between the quantitatively perfect symmetry of two halves and their poorly matched, forcibly stitched contents that makes "The Elephant Vanishes" at once unique and awkward as a text. On the one hand, the text divided exactly at the midpoint largely precludes a possibility of a mere chance. Although Saitō Tomoya argues that the protagonist might be telling his entire narrative to the reader from the standpoint at its closure (Saitō 83, 91–92), he is hardly capable of or inclined to provide such a carefully measured narration when he growingly fails to suppress mental disequilibrium in the end. Rather, it suggests an incisive authorial intervention.

On the other hand, the two sections not only do not interrelate well in content, but they are also structurally ill-fitted with each other. Consisting of the narrator's voice and his observations, the first section is given exclusively in the first-person narration, while the second section mixes dialogues with the first-person narration. The first section can stand almost independently on its own as one of Murakami's weird short stories with a kind of closure that comes with people's fading interest in the elephant, whereas the second section topically depends on the first half for its unfolding, and the narrative remains open-ended without a resolution regarding what becomes of the narrator. The text as a whole might give us the impression of an inadequately crafted, even ill-conceived composition.

In fact, the topic of the elephant's disappearance, which is one of the only two elements found in the two sections, provides a certain common thread in terms of economic expediency. In a word, the animal metaphorically embodies unwanted existence, and therefore it shrinks and disappears as expected. The town's adoption and care of the otherwise helpless animal appears benevolently considerate enough, and the local citizenry, including the narrator, generally welcomes the notion of a town-owned elephant as their shared property. But the elephant's presence is actually not quite appreciated as the costless ways to keep it alive attest to. The municipal administration would rather not suffer the infamy of elephant killing or incur tax revenue loss due to the hampered construction of a high-rise condominium on the former zoo site. As a political compromise for saving their face and money, the town takes over the elephant for free. The real estate developer pays for enclosing facilities and donates a small lot at the hilly outskirts where an old school gym is moved to shelter the animal. The elephant keeper is still paid by his previous employer, and the creature mainly feeds on schoolchildren's lunch leftovers.

Furthermore, the visitor finds the animal solidly tied to the concrete base with an unbreakably thick and sturdy iron chain and fenced in with concrete and large iron bars about three meters high. Large and powerful as an elephant is, this is obviously an excessive security measure against the "feeble old thing" that is considered not "likely to pose a danger to anyone" (310, 311).[8] Nobody objects to this rather harsh treatment, however, and the aged creature is expected to pass away sooner than later. In fact, the municipal government anticipates "tak[ing] full possession of the land" upon the animal's death that should occur in the near future (311). As the narrator suspects some causality between people's perception of the elephant and their swift consignment of its memory into oblivion, the creature's abrupt disappearance amounts to no more than what is supposed to happen before long, actually rendering the whole process less troublesome or costly for those in charge by not leaving a huge carcass to dispose of. The incident is "convenient to all the sides . . . even their unspoken desire" (Wada 163). The old, quiet, reserved keeper with almost round, disproportionally large ears, whom alone the elephant trusts wholeheartedly, and vice versa, symbolically stands for an extension of the animal and, as such, disappears with it.

In this case, the old elephant together with its keeper in the first half of the story epitomizes uselessness as a being that proves totally inefficient in enhancing any social productivity. As the narrator observes, their disappearance has brought forth no change whatsoever in the workings of society. In Murakami's fictional world, along with cats and sheep, elephants often appear, as illustrated by another short story titled "*Odoru kobito* 踊る小人 (The Dancing Dwarf)" (1984) in which a large factory complex manufactures a monthly set number of live copies of an elephant with a kind of biotechnology to meet popular demand. In *The Wind-Up Bird Chronicle*, thanks to their sheer size, two elephants are spared from the "liquidat[ion]" of supposedly threatening, large zoo animals by imperial Japanese troops in the Manchurian capital city of Hsin-ching at the end of World War II.[9]

In "The Elephant Vanishes," however, even such a favorite creature is not immune from a fate that arrives without much delay, once one is deemed useless and unneeded, analogous to what happens to "bears and tigers and leopards and wolves" in the Manchurian zoo (*Chronicle* [1997a] 410), or to what ultimately befalls the protagonist of Kafka's *Metamorphosis*. Unlike those creatures, the old elephant apparently accepts its own extinction without resistance or even "gladly" into "a different, chilling kind of" dimension (326). Notwithstanding, the pivotal, normative concept here is efficiency, or, as Jean-François Lyotard's puts, "performativity—that is, the best possible input/output equation" (Lyotard 46), in the highly advanced stage of capitalism that always prescribes the social milieu of Murakami's fiction. The "performativity" of a zoo animal is low to begin with, consisting of some aesthetic, sentimental value thanks to its exotic appeal. The "input/output equation" of the aged elephant in question is nil or minimal, if any, perhaps except for the townspeople's self-satisfaction for keeping the feeble creature alive, but their kind gesture thinly veils the underlying anticipation of its fast-approaching demise. As Wada argues, we should sense "the presence of force that, innate to our own world, suppresses heterogeneous excess."[10]

This point of efficiency in part helps to bring together the ill-related two sections of the story, for the narrator's life as a PR official in the second half centers on it both in personal philosophy and for corporate success, illustrated by his dwelling use of *yōryōyoku* 要領よく (effectually) and *bengi-teki/sei* 便宜的／性 (convenient/convenience, expedient/expediency).[11] At the business party, he promotes a newly produced set of kitchen appliances, the important aspect of which, he stresses to the editor he has just met, is its impeccable coordination in color, design, and function. As the main selling point of the products, "simplicity, functionality, unity" in this context easily translate into efficiency or performativity (*Zen sakuhin* 8 [1991] 51). In order to enhance his sales pitch as instructed by the company, the narrator insists on using the English word *kitchen* that presumably sounds more stylish and alluring than its Japanese counterpart. Although he privately admits that the kitchen needs a few other features than unity, he rejects them as unmarketable, extending the idea to "this pragmatic (*bengi-teki-na*) world of ours" in which "things you can't sell don't count for much" (320; *Zen sakuhin* 8 [1991] 51). He concludes the argument by saying that everybody thinks the same, despite the woman's skepticism. By pursuing the way of the world as he understands it, the narrator greatly succeeds as a salesperson of kitchen appliances, even "in selling myself to" people (327).

Thus, the two divided halves are linked to each other through the notion of economic expediency. This, however, brings into light a few issues concerning the other common element, the narrator-protagonist. First, although he provides the narrating voice about his interest in the elephant and belief in efficiency, he scarcely tells us anything else about what constitutes his personal being, such as his upbringing, social activities, and especially his inner thoughts and self-reflections. Second, it is incongruous for an able professional like him to have exhibited "from the very outset" (310) a keen, constant interest in an old elephant, which, as a very embodiment of unsalability, should have nothing to do with him. Nonetheless, he regularly comes to see the animal on weekends, often from a rear hillside vantage point that he alone knows. When asked, he admits that he has liked elephants as far as he remembers, but he cannot provide a reason for his sustained, even unusual fascination with them. Last, for all his assertion of pragmatism and personal success in marketability and efficiency, we find him unsure of his mental equilibrium and unable to attune himself well to the external world at the end of the story. Altogether, these points put into question what kind of person he is, although he appears like a normal resident of the town.

With regard to the narrator's unspecified internal life, there can be two possible explanations. He either carefully avoids divulging what ruminates in his mind or simply does not have much inner thought on a conscious level. The first possibility would render him a keenly self-conscious intellectual who knows what to reveal in his narration selectively from personal observations and experiences, in order to conceal what privately matters most from anyone who has access to his narration. This is not very likely, however, considering the fact that the narrator does not address the reader. Apparently unaware of, or neglecting the presence of readership that follows his story, he does not show any necessity to hide aspects of his life, private as well as public, in personal accounts that are devoid of internal deliberations in spite of good intellect, abilities, and certain knowledge at his disposal. He just keeps on talking about his observations and what transpires with the editor. We are then left with the alternative explanation.

As pointed out above, his professional belief in efficiency for economic advantage does not accord with his persistent interest in a senile animal. He even betrays such a close sense of affinity and sympathy with it as to personify the animal with *hitori* 一人 [*Zen sakuhin* 8 (1991) 41], a counter reserved for a human being, when it is left alone in the bankrupt zoo, while he does ridicule with emphatic dots the newspaper's usage of *hitogara* 人柄 about its "personal character" (*Zen sakuhin* 8 [1991] 48). He might be strongly fascinated by the elephant precisely because it represents an antipode of the performative value he ostensibly upholds, when he actually harbors an unacknowledged doubt and apprehension about the pursuit of efficiency that even commodifies him.[12] He is, after all, no more than an able, yet little self-reflective salesperson. Complacent as he is about his marketing prowess, he nevertheless retains some humanly inefficient traits unstifled, unlike the Boss's precise, power-driven secretary in *A Wild Sheep Chase* who, devoid of emotional superfluity, purely incarnates efficiency in Murakami's entire fiction.

Against his own reason, the narrator in "The Elephant Vanishes" has to feel, without realizing it, certain misgivings about the relentless pursuit of efficiency, because that means to deprive him of any inefficient elements, including human attributes like desire for an interpersonal relationship. This is why he inexplicably feels most attracted to watching the elephant unreservedly interacting with the keeper in the evening when they show their mutual, brimming trust and affection in privacy. In his own case, he fails to bring the burgeoning acquaintance with the young editor to a next, intimate stage when he inadvertently divulges a secret of the elephant vanishing, thereby stirring up the core of his insecurity, of which he is not well aware. In his own words, he initially succeeds in adroitly *selling himself to* her with his professional refinement, and yet he is then unable to deal with the emergent inner demon that forms an integral part of what he has become thanks to that excellent performativity. In the end, he loses interest in continuing the relationship, because he innately feels uncertain and futile about applying his philosophy of constantly seeking the most advantageous cause-and-effect outcome to anything new in his life outside of what his job calls for.

In a rare, yet hesitant and passing self-analysis, the narrator retrospectively ascribes the indiscreet mention of such "a topic the most improper" for the first dating, which he immediately regrets, to an "unconscious" urge to tell someone about his secret (*Zen sakuhin* 8 [1991] 53). His psychological uneasiness also manifests itself in the fact that he picks up a smoking habit again after three years when the elephant disappears. He lights a cigarette at two strained moments during the conversation with the editor, once when she challenges him about his unhesitant assertion of the world's expedient nature, which he immediately admits he does not entirely believe in. Then, aware that she detects "unnaturally distorted chilliness" in his initial attempt to steer their topic away from the elephant (*Zen sakuhin* 8 [1991] 53), he has recourse to another cigarette.

Encountering difficulties in understanding his elusive explanation, she rightly figures out that the problem lies not in her but in him, while he still does not acknowledge the serious nature of his problem. The woman, who has already expressed her reservation about his unabashed advocacy for marketability, senses his unspoken trouble fermenting inside at the mention of the elephant and instinctively refrains from further personal involvement. As Murakami states, the female character in his fiction often functions as a medium through which "something happen[s]" and "visions . . . are shown" to the male protagonist ("Art of Fiction" [2004b] 133).[13] She elicits a problem surrounding or inherent in her male counterpart so that he can finally become aware of the nature and gravity of the situation. In this case, the editor achieves the effect by insisting on hearing about the narrator's secret of the vanished elephant.[14] Whether or not the male protagonist can make proper use of the opportunity to deal with his problem hinges on his willingness to understand, accept, and act on the revealed knowledge. This brings us back to the question of what kind of person our narrator-protagonist is.

Murakami's first-person male narrators before the turn of the century tend to have a kind of regular or temporary employments that require certain intellectual finesse but do not produce anything very tangible or lasting at, for instance, an advertising agency or a corporation's PR department. In a sense, this kind of works in their purest form are ideal in terms of efficiency because they do not involve raw, physical materials while labor outputs are thoroughly consumed at the moment of production. These professionals thrive on the forefront of informational, service-oriented economy, but they might share an uncertain basis of existence largely due to the very nature of their work. The narrator in "The Elephant Vanishes" belongs to this group as an outstanding marketer.

The problem is that he does not make conscious efforts to closely examine and understand his own issues. In this respect, he resembles his counterparts in the sister short stories of the 1980s. As we have seen in the previous chapter, struck by a painfully ravenous hunger, the narrator-protagonist in "The Second Bakery Attack," who works for a law firm, is coerced into *attacking* a McDonald's with his wife in the middle of a night without daring to comprehend a fundamental cause or a reason in him. In "TV People" as we venture next, the narrator-protagonist, employed in the marketing department of a major electronics corporation, similarly cannot deal with shrunken people intrusively carrying a TV set into segments of his private and public life. There is a crucial difference, however, between these main figures and the one in "The Elephant Vanishes."

In the other two stories, the unnamed protagonists at least realize, albeit vaguely, a serious problem latent in them through visualizing it with a metaphorical image. As we have seen, the protagonist in "The Second Bakery Attack" introduces the image of an undersea dormant volcano to explain his mental situation under duress from the irrepressible hunger and his importunate wife. He fearfully observes the imagined volcano through the too transparent water on which his vicarious self is floating in a small boat. After a few encounters with shrunken TV People just over one day, the protagonist in "TV People" has a vivid dream in which all his office colleagues in a business meeting are turned dead into stone statues. Upon awakening, he senses himself also losing speech and getting petrified from the fingertips, and the transformation is actually befalling him in real life at the end of the story. These two characters do not fully understand the significance of their respective images, but they are at least aware that their underlying fear confronts them in a clear, highly symbolic visual representation.

This is not the case with their counterpart in "The Elephant Vanishes." The narrator fails to visualize a problem either passively in a dream or by actively exerting imagination. The closest he can get to that state of visual realization takes place at the very end of the first section. Just before the break between the two halves, for a few months even after the elephant's disappearance, he often visits the empty enclosure that used to house the animal, only to find the place somewhat unnatural and desolate each time. Antithetical as the visits are to his belief in economic efficiency, he nevertheless repeats them, compelled by an incomprehensible drive from within. The very fact that he chooses to come back to see the empty space multiple times suggests its relevance to his hardly self-examined problem.

This scene of an unoccupied enclosure turns out highly significant in deciphering the story, for Murakami, who often gets motivated to write a novel with the conception of an initial scene or image,[15] ascribes the inception of this story to his creative curiosity about an imagined "elephant house from which the elephant has disappeared."[16] The bleak landscapes that give a sense of decay and desolation recur in his fiction. Examples include the aforementioned dream scene in "TV People" and the remote, hard-to-reach location in the midst of Hokkaido where the narrator-protagonist of *A Wild Sheep Chase* waits alone for an encounter with the unknown just before snow closes the passage out. In *Hard-Boiled Wonderland and the End of the World*, through a botched cerebral experiment, an almost deserted, walled town operates in the mind separately from the surface consciousness, with an effect of making its inhabitants lose their previous memories. In each of these cases, the forlorn location corresponds to a mind in which humanness is somehow being impaired or endangered, while at the same time providing the protagonist with a rare, last chance to recognize and address his problem. The narrator in "TV People" realizes it but does not have time to deal with it. The one in *A Wild Sheep Chase* undergoes a reunion with his deceased friend as a lingering double of teenage days only to go back to his regular life in the end, bereft of the last remnants of his youth as a result. The *Boku* 僕 (I) in "The End of the World" does figure out his problem and takes an action.

It is relevant to notice here that all the abovementioned characters find themselves within some kinds of enclosure, and the closed spaces can be their starting point for self-renewal, if they actually realize their situations and make efforts to get out of the impasse that is rather mental than spatial. In this respect, *The Wind-Up Bird Chronicle* typifies a successful case. Its protagonist named Okada Toru repeatedly goes down into a dark, lifeless, closed space of a dry well for days. A crucial difference is that he stays at the bottom of an empty well with his own will and embraces hours of physical duress each time, urged by a mounting sense of need to deal with a difficulty inherent in his life. As a result of intense self-contemplation in subterranean utter darkness, he manages to commune with the spiritual essence of his lost wife and defeat his evil brother-in-law through a nonphysical channel before he emerges from the well for the last time, severely bruised and yet expectant of a new phase of his life.

This self-examination often accompanied by the act of symbolically passing into one's innermost psyche is also an important, recurring motif in Murakami's works. Okada voluntarily goes down to the bottom of the dry well. The teenage protagonist in *Kafka on the Shore* encounters a rarefied locus of his unconscious, Oedipal desires when he ventures deep into the mythically impenetrable, dense forest of Shikoku. In *1Q84*, Aomame, the female protagonist whose orbit of action is separated from that of the male counterpart in alternate chapters, finally gets reunited with her soul mate after her descent into a parallel world. In fact, the importance of symbolic passage, usually in the form of physical descent into an enclosed space, extends to, and stems from the author himself when he metaphorically compares his method of conceiving a novel to going down into a hidden, dark, underground area of the house at the risk of never returning or jeopardizing his sanity.[17]

It follows that facing the external void that interests him irresistibly must be the very situation in which the narrator-protagonist in "The Elephant Vanishes" could delve into the deeper realm of his mind to look for a cause of what has been unsettling him for a long time. Not daring or able to undertake such a close self-examination, however, he misses a precious opportunity to confront the cause. All he does is to keep on gazing repeatedly, and he does not undergo any transformation or take any action in the face of the closed blank space. Lacking in mental power or capacity other than practical intellect, he is even less inclined than the other protagonists to expose himself to risky self-exploration, maintaining, instead, the status quo of ever-growing applicability of efficiency as if mnemonically programmed. Thus, the story at the very end aptly shows him still observing the empty enclosure that looks even more desolate with the coming winter, which mirrors his own internal wastes.

In a metaphoric sense, the narrator-protagonist's humanity strongly corresponds to the ancient elephant in terms of inefficiency. Regarded as an unneeded, cumbersome burden, nominally receiving recognition for social decency, yet largely neglected, it is very much enfeebled while deprived of freedom by way of a thick chain of his purely utilitarian thinking.[18] This metaphorical affinity accounts for his otherwise inexplicable attraction to the animal from the onset. Without knowing it, he innately feels threatened by his own relentless pursuit of efficiency that sacrifices his human nature, and he finds an equivalent symbol of his endangered humanity in the aged elephant. According to the unnamed narrator-protagonist in *Notes from Underground* (1864) by Fyodor Dostoevsky, whom Murakami admires as a novelist along with Kafka as already mentioned in foreword and chapter 3, what makes us human in an increasingly positivistic society is our willful desire for the irrational against our own calculated advantage. Murakami's narrator here opts for the irrational, the inefficient, which goes against his principle of numerable gains at the least costs possible. Unmediated as his visits might be to the deserted elephant house, they are likely his last-ditch attempt at holding onto his sense of humanity and mind's stability.

The narrator's fundamental problem is threefold. First, placed outside of the enclosure, he is not at the right place to start with, because he cannot free himself when he is not confined, physically or symbolically. Metaphorically speaking, his humanity is, but that is not allowed autonomous agency unlike *Boku*'s Shadow in "The End of the World." The narrator has no power or opportunity to alter his own situation as a result. Instead, the elephant as his metaphorical correlative is in bondage. Second, with the elephant gone, he has even lost an object to correlate with, forced to live with the void left by the animal's physical disappearance outside and his consequently diminishing humanity inside. These two factors keep him in psychological suspense for months, until he is driven toward a mental breakdown when the precarious balance between his increasing business success and reduced humanness is finally tipped at the brink of collapse. Third, despite an indefinably palpable apprehension as discussed above, content with his rising professional fortune on the conscious level, he is neither able nor willing to examine an underlying situation in order to get himself out of life's mounting crisis.

In this context, the blank space that separates the text's two sections indicates far more than a mere lapse of several months. Although, generally speaking, such an inserted passage of time might suggest a certain change taking place in the story, the current case points to the narrator's stalemate in understanding and motivating himself toward a new direction. Textually, the blank space that follows the vacant enclosure on the page is a physical embodiment and a symbolic carryover of the spiritual stagnation. Of greater significance here, however, is the undeclared, yet irreconcilably sharp contrast between the character's incapability and irresolution for self-renewal and the author's decisive, if not deliberate intervention in incisively dividing the story in the very middle.

The exact division of two sections might be expected to separate one aspect of the narrator-protagonist's life from another. Indeed, we find the narrator in the first section meticulously tracing the social unfolding of the elephant incident all by himself mostly in the private space of his apartment, while the second section presents him in his public function through his interaction with the magazine editor. The disconnect appears to ensure the private and public spheres of his life being set apart clearly as the narrator undoubtedly intends them not to affect each other. Like many of Murakami's other protagonists in the 1980s, he is "not a 'self-closed' youth but an individual" who "tries to live through 'the advanced capitalistic society' all by himself . . . with complete 'autonomy'" (Kawamoto 15).

In human terms, however, an attempt at such strict, clear-cut demarcation hardly succeeds, especially when one carries psychological uncertainty. Thus, far from being suppressed, the genuine concern that the narrator evinces about the elephant's fate in the first half resurfaces later when, against his best judgment and qualms, he confides the source of his insecurity to the female editor in spite of his professed rationalism of marketability. Therefore, an inefficient, yet essential element of human weakness links the two sharply divided halves different in nature, when the narrator is not in a mental state to resolutely address his trouble. It is the authorial design that creates an unstable text with irrationality unpreventably spilling over the borderline of geometric partition, and the resulting story indicates the predicament of postindustrial people who are expected to live as efficiently as possible even to the detriment of their overall integrity as human beings.

The titles of the original Japanese text and its English translation implicitly happen to stand for different aspects of this short story. The noun-phrased Japanese title, 象の消滅, which literally means the extinction of an elephant, addresses a definite, "too complete" (321, 326), irreversible state of nonbeing as the animal has already ceased to exist before the story begins to delineate its circumstances. By contrast, the verbal English title not only denotes an active process of the elephant's gradual disappearance in the narrator's account but also alludes to the ensuing change in him as his anxiety progressively develops, ultimately leaving him in a habitually dazed condition of skewed perception and judgment. Even when he finally suspects a cause in himself, he nevertheless does not dare to examine it. The text ends without suggesting any means by which he might elude an impending mental breakdown amid his rising marketing success. He still comes to see the vacant enclosure covered with dead weed in approaching winter without expecting any possibility of its former occupants' return.

When Murakami delivered an acceptance speech for the International Catalunya Prize on June 9, 2011, he rhetorically posed a question about the cause of the nuclear reactor meltdowns that had taken place in Fukushima, Japan, three months earlier. The inhabitants in nearby towns were forced to flee, and the immediate areas have remained deserted since. Rather than ascribing the disaster to natural forces, he found a ready answer in the post–World War II pursuit of *efficiency* for a supposedly secure, inexpensive source of energy by the collective will of corporations, the government, and ultimately the people, including himself, who consumed that supply of power in comfort and, as such, became "at once victims and victimizers" of the disaster ("*Katarūnya*" [2011b]; see also *Shokugyō* [2015] 202–4, 212). This is a recent example of the deep-rooted distrust of *the system* that he has sustained and expressed for decades,[19] at least since the days of student demonstrations in the late 1960s.

As Kawakami Chiyoko argues, the target of Murakami's critique might not be so easily identifiable with "a unified ideological entity" of the authoritative institution like a reactionary government as it used to be for writers of older generations (Kawakami 310). It is largely because he is fundamentally opposed to an amorphous, immense complex of desire for power, sociopolitical control over individuality, and an ever more *efficient* flow of capital that, if left unchecked, seeks to exploit individuals to their detriment. This *system* might likely include those very individuals as unknowing accomplices, illustrating one aspect of Jamesonian postmodernity cited in the previous chapter above (Jameson 49; see also Kawamoto 22). In his personal life, Murakami appears to exemplify the condition when, unlike his poverty-stricken younger days, he has fulfilled the desire of possessing or consuming certain objects, such as an impressive collection of CDs, records, and other items of luxury, with a prospering writing career. Unlike characters of his making who unquestioningly tend to embrace overflowing consumables or "the trivia of contemporary urban life" (Rubin [1992] 494; see also Kawakami 320–323), however, he has consciously, almost inveterately kept the critical "distance from it" in another part of his mind (Jameson 49), and that critical gaze manifests itself in many of his writings.

Murakami might not appear to "confront the age directly" according to Kawamoto Saburō. But this does not mean that he "quietly accepts the system . . . with all its contradictions" (Kawamoto 19–20), as we have seen that "The Elephant Vanishes" demonstrates to the contrary. While containing such contradictions, his overall stance as a novelist continues to problematize them, especially in the fiction he creates. Although deviating from what Jameson speculates on, his unwavering critical stance reveals innate, quiet, yet inextinguishable rage against *the system* in postmodern reality.

In the style of apparent irrelevance and lighthearted playfulness with no straightforward meaning, Murakami touches upon vaguely felt dangers latent in individual life of today's society. In Lyotard's terms, he "puts forward the unpresentable in presentation itself" by "invent[ing] allusions to the conceivable which cannot be presented" (Lyotard 81). Or, as Jameson phrases more specifically, the Japanese writer has created a story that is "'irrational' in the older sense of 'incomprehensible'" in an age that almost precludes such irrationality, pointing to the "enormous and threatening, yet only dimly perceivable, other reality of economic and social institutions" (Jameson 268, 38).

In the next chapter, we will further explore the nature of the world in which we live, this time with the focus on the relationship between humanity and the technology of the electronic media as presented in Murakami's "TV People."

NOTES

1. Rubin (1996), who is one of the two translators of the pieces included in *The Elephant Vanishes*, ascribes its final edited form to the liking of an editor at Alfred A. Knopf that originally published the collection (63–64).

2. Nakamura 109. In discussion of the motif of disappearance in Murakami's fiction, especially *The Wind-Up Bird Chronicle*, Nakamura (109) further explains this

idea as "media as a message in which the message content is nullified, that is, a pure significant."

3. For summaries of sampled criticism, see Kawakami 310–12, 320; Rubin (1992) 499.

4. See a short list in Nakamura 107. Wada (160) argues that we would be able to make "a quite lengthy, complicated list . . . of things lost" in Murakami's stories.

5. "Zō no shōmetsu," in Pan'ya saishūgeki (*The Second Bakery Attack*) (1986) 35–62.

6. "The Elephant Vanishes," trans. Jay Rubin, in *The Elephant Vanishes* (1993) 308–27.

7. In the case of this text contained in *Murakami Haruki zen sakuhin 1979–1989 8* (1991), the second section is slightly longer, probably due to the transcription of the dialogue with which the second section abounds unlike the first.

8. Unless otherwise noted, all the references to this short story are to its translation by Jay Rubin in *The Elephant Vanishes* (1993).

9. *The Wind-Up Bird Chronicle*, trans. Jay Rubin (1997a) 409, 410. All the references to this novel are to this translation. Hisai and Kuwa (112–35) trace Murakami's use of elephants from his earliest novel through the 1980s with the viewpoint that he gave "a negative image as a sign" to the animals from the beginning (Hisai and Kuwa 131). They, however, dismiss the two early short stories in which elephants play a crucial role, "The Elephant Vanishes" and "The Dancing Dwarf," as unimportant and fail to discuss their significance.

10. Wada 163. Through his Internet research of newspaper articles during the decade from late 1980s to late 1990s, Wada (162–63) further argues that, apart from the difficulty in reproducing them, elephants in Japanese zoos "have become being eliminated due to their economic [in]efficiency . . . even better to disappear . . . for their excessive size." Murakami makes this point even more apparent by having his elephant very old in the story.

11. *Murakami Haruki zen sakuhin 1979–1989 8* (1991) 50–52, 60. All the references to this short story in the original are to this edition, and their translation is mine.

12. As Saitō (86) argues, the narrator's meticulous attention to numbers, especially in the passage of time, might be "a manifestation of excessive attempt to adapt to 'reality' by [him] who holds 'incompatibility with reality' like harboring 'personal interest' in an elephant."

13. See also "Sean Wilsey" (2005b) 247 as well as the beginning of his short story, "Rēdāhōzen レーダーホーゼン (Lederhosen)" (1985), as an example. As the author, Murakami (2015) even acknowledges indebtedness more to his female characters than to male ones for guiding him in fiction writing (*Shokugyō* [2015] 232–35).

14. In this respect, she functions like the female spousal figure in "The Second Bakery Attack" as discussed in the previous chapter.

15. For instance, the short story "*Nejimakidori to kayōbi no onnatachi* ねじまき鳥と火曜日の女たち (The Wind-Up Bird and Tuesday's Women)" (1986) obviously paved the way for the much longer novel *The Wind-Up Bird Chronicle* that came out eight years later. See also Mori Mayumi.

16. Hisai and Kuwa 129. They cite this remark from an interview with Murakami in the Japanese edition of the *Playboy* magazine (May 1986).

17. See "*écrire*" (2003b) 99–100; "In Dreams Begins" (2005d) 558–59; *Hashiru koto* (2007a) 133–37; *Shokugyō* (2015) 175–76.

18. To a certain extent, the metaphor might also apply to the Humanities of today's academia for their institutional plight in such countries as Japan and the United States.

19. For typical examples, see "Jerusalem Prize" (2009c) and *Shokugyō* (2015) 97, 200–2. The narrator's unwillingness and inability to reflect on the cause of his own predicament coincidentally prefigures Japan's attempts at gradual resumption of nuclear power generation just a few years after the earthquake-caused tsunami destroyed the nuclear plant.

Chapter 6

"TV People"
The Slick Assault by Electronic Media

"TV pīpuru TVピープル (TV People)" (1989) presents an exceptional, if not unique, case in Murakami's fiction in the sense that, in this short story, technology assumes central importance. The technology in question, which is the analogue TV system, has already been outdated and replaced by the digitized counterpart for a few decades, but the significance of this work still lies in problematizing the relationship between humans and technology, starting with the writer's own case. Far from being a mere "bad dream, an optical illusion" (Monnet 357), the story critiques the fundamental ways televisual and electronic media in general affect people's life, the most important of which concerns the dismantlement of the autonomous self as a pivotal sociocultural construct of intellectual endeavor.

As a writer of contemporaneity, Murakami has made extensive public use of the Internet system four times so far, accepting and answering many questions from his readers in Japan and abroad through a temporary website, publishing select collections of correspondence in the form of books and extended versions as CD-ROMs or an electronic book.[1] Although this occasional practice calls for strenuous efforts at the expense of his other writing activities, he considers it an important means to have direct contact with his readership rather than a relatively quick, lucrative form of publication. The undertakings prove his Internet literacy. Curiously, this online familiarity on a personal level does not translate well into the scarcity of references to information technology in his fiction, and they are far dispersed and not always of the latest kind. Examples include the cassette tape and its recorder that the narrator in "*Kangarū tsūshin* カンガルー通信 (The Kangaroo Communiqué)" (1981) uses and the online conversation with keyboard typing via the telephone line between protagonist and his brother-in-law, as well as his missing wife in *The Wind-Up Bird Chronicle*.

At least in creating his fictional world, Murakami appears rather reluctant to incorporate the latest technology of communication, as exemplified by *1Q84*. With the alphabet *Q* pronounced the same as the number 9 in Japanese, the very title indicates the story's time frame clearly set in the year of 1984, like George Orwell's *Nineteen Eighty-Four* (1949) to which it pays titular homage. Like the British dystopian counterpart, Murakami's story somewhat affiliates itself with science fiction when the term 1Q84 refers to a parallel world that one of the main characters, Aomame, inadvertently slips into. Unlike Orwell's novel that features imaginary technology of ubiquitous surveillance devices from the futuristic viewpoint of the 1940s, however, Murakami's novel, published a quarter century after the story's dated setting, realistically refers to the technology that was available in the mid-1980s. The deliberately reversed lapse of time suggests at once Murakami's comfort with writing about earlier in his lifetime and his discomfort to fully negotiate the current Internet-based, informational society.

To a lesser degree, this temporal scheme suggestive of the writer's hesitation to incorporate up-to-date technology also applies to *Killing Commendatore* (2017) that draws back about a decade earlier for its main setting instead of addressing the present time of its actual writing later in the mid-2010s. Accordingly, the characters customarily use cellular phones, but smartphones have not made their debut as yet, even in this latest novel. Meanwhile, the reclusive character Menshiki accesses the Internet with "a laptop" and "a state-of-the-art Apple desktop computer" at his isolated residence among hills.[2] Generally speaking, Murakami's fiction centers on human affairs that have little to do with the advancing forefront of technology for communication, relying instead on established kinds, such as radio, LP, CD, and TV, as staple elements of the social fabric from his young days.

This noncommitment to advanced technology contrasts to, for instance, Kazuo Ishiguro's stance. Born five years apart shortly after World War II, Ishiguro (1954–) and Murakami respect each other as contemporary writers of international standing. Like the Japanese counterpart, the British writer is not known to avidly pursue new or emerging technology, with one major exception of *Never Let Me Go* (2005), which anticipated the nationalized system of human clone production to medically harvest organs in the foreseeable future. This novel was probably inspired by the world's first cloned animal, Dolly the sheep, in July of 1996, and it was hardly a coincidence for the novel to come out of the United Kingdom, where the sensationally innovative, biological experiment successfully took place. While uplifting national pride, the scientific breakthrough immediately stirred up the prospect of eventual human cloning with varying consequences, mostly of a genetically bleak future.

It is apparent that Murakami's creative mind does not concern itself very much with what evolving technology signifies for humanity.[3] Outside of information technology, *Hard-Boiled Wonderland and the End of the World* might seem to present an anomalous case, but its purely imaginary cerebral experiment that creates an autonomous subconscious world was not grounded on an existing or emerging technology of the 1980s reality. "TV People," therefore, stands out among his fictional pieces all the more for its focus on one of the most widespread, modern technological phenomena. The short story deserves close attention for that reason alone, inciting a basic question as to what underlies an apparently nonsensical story about intruders from the other side of television.

Although Murakami's fiction has enjoyed high popularity in many parts of the world for decades, certain established writers and critics have not tended to regard it favorably. For instance, while online bookmakers and news organizations have not failed to mention his name as one of the top candidates for a Nobel Prize for Literature every fall in recent years, the selection committee has always proven to have different criteria. A major reason lies in the nature of his writings. Usually written in an easy style to read, and filled with original humor, unrealistic occurrences, and references to consumer goods and items of popular culture, they are prone to inviting criticism of frivolity and irrelevance by those who regard noticeably grave, sociopolitical conditions as a novelist's foremost duty to cope with. From another perspective, however, Murakami addresses certain contemporary issues in his own way as I argued in previous chapters. The unreal content, for example, is in fact akin to works of Kafka and magical realism, alluding to a hardly articulable problem that lurks in the psyche or society, through unconventional, sometimes shocking representation. His fiction thus confounds the boundary between serious and popular kinds of literature, to which "TV People" testifies well.

The story does not abide by logic or reason in realistic terms, sounding almost as if the author enjoyed perplexing the reader with its nonsensical content. Indeed, the text exhibits a strong sense of playfulness in several respects. The sudden, inexplicable intrusion of shrunken people with a TV set into the narrator-protagonist's daily routine, as well as one of them coming out of TV in the end, indicates a major element of humor on the plot level. On the sensuous level, soon after the story's beginning, the reader encounters transcriptions of the noises that the narrator hears of a clock in the living room and a stranger's reverberating footsteps outside. Those supposed onomatopoeia in writing forcibly attract the reader's attention audio-visually because they stand out on the pages for their jarring, consonant-rich formations that are hard to pronounce, as well as for their emphatic presentations with bold letters in the original Japanese text and with whole capitalization in the English translation. With no semblance to any regular clock sounds or footsteps, the transcriptions are obviously meant to be word plays on the surface. Word play is also apparent when the narrator explains the strange, yet barely noticeable deviation of TV People's physique that is proportionally reduced by 20 to 30 percent in relation to the normal human size. To express their reduced body, the text repeats the brief sentence, "That's TV People," three times in ever smaller font sizes (198).[4]

With regard to consumer or popular items, apart from frequent mentions of TV, this story has a number of references to magazines targeted for young to middle-aged women with disposable incomes, such as *Elle* エル, *Marie Claire* マリ・クレール, *an・an* アンアン, *Croissant* クロワッサン, and *Katei gahō* 家庭画報, which is translated as *Home Ideas*. For her editorial research and personal interests, the narrator's wife subscribes to the periodicals, the latest issues of which she organizes in a pile on the sideboard of their living room. The husband does not care for them in the slightest, even wishing for the thorough elimination of all the world's magazines. Accepting their presence in his domestic surroundings as part of his marital condition, however, he confesses to the fear of disturbing the orderly pile of magazines lest that act of negligence provoke the displeasure of his meticulous wife. Magazines by nature are produced as consumables for an easy pastime and quick information, and their presence in the story bespeaks the consumption-oriented popular culture in which it is set.

The origin of "TV People" might also account, in part at least, for an ambience of playful creativity through its close affinity with popular culture and consumer society. In the late 1980s when Murakami languished in inertia after having completed two long novels, including *Norwegian Wood* and *Dance Dance Dance*, he was suddenly inspired to write the short story "almost automatically," after he watched on MTV "the video clip of Lou Reed's song," in which "two strangely dressed men were carrying a large box all over the town."[5] The video helped him to break the writer's block.

With an uneasy, foreboding tone that is far from light-hearted and merely amusing, however, the short story points to certain problems inherent in the very normal way we live our television-saturated lives. The intrusion of TV-carrying people into one's life, for instance, stands for the omnipresence of electronic media in every corner of the society that seeks easy access to entertainment and information. The salience of their obtrusive visits aligns itself with the media's influence, so pervasive and prevalent as to affect even those who, like the narrator, have opted out of televisual exposure. At the same time, with their uniformly plain, impersonally nondescript appearance and their silent team maneuver not interfering with the general population, TV People integrate themselves into the social background so thoroughly that they do not attract attention or suspicion from anyone other than the narrator, because people willingly embrace the media's availability for their convenience and take it for granted as an indispensable part of their lives.

"TV People" thus reveals how the television system affects people significantly through unhindered infiltration into society and solid placement in it as a presumed necessity. Certain kinds of exhibited humor might entertain the reader without offering much reason to laugh outright, while supposedly facilitating the text to deliver its social commentary. The text ill qualifies as a conventional satirical piece of dark humor, however, because the oblique presentation heavily muffles and even distorts an assumed message to hamper and confuse understanding. Little attenuated negativity is the overall effect until the very end, when the story offers not so much an open ending as an ambiguous resolution of alternative demises. For the sake of quick nomenclature, one might be tempted to ascribe such a composition to postmodern playful disillusionment with reality. In fact, the story delves into an even more fundamental predicament that besets and undermines today's humanity beyond mere technophobia, which essentially accounts for the looming sense of negativity.

Rather than suggesting imaginable possibilities to evolve after the textual closure, the ending in question presents an interpretive impasse with mutually entangled, multiple combinations of dead ends. First, finding himself somewhat getting dry and shrunken toward the end of his narration, the narrator fears impending death through petrification like what his office colleagues have undergone in his short dream immediately before one of the TV People emerges out of the TV. That is an awareness of physical death, on the one hand. In the overall context of repeated emphasis on the reduced size of TV People, on the other hand, the perceived physical shrinkage might indicate the narrator's mutation into a nonhuman form of such people (see Monnet 341, 343, 357). Their persistent interest in him as a target of their invasion might bespeak their unspoken intention to enlarge their cohort. The absence of a single, definite outcome does not make it clear whether he is becoming another of them or turning into stone at the end. More importantly, in either case, he is at a loss what to say, because he is losing capability to not only vocalize but also form his own thought, which amounts to the loss of his mental faculties and signifies the demise of his internal being.

Second, the one that steps out of the screen and has apparent leadership over the other two TV People makes two predictive statements. First, he declares twice in close proximity that the narrator's wife, who has mysteriously failed to come home that evening, will no longer return to him (奥さんは帰ってこないよ).[6] Then, he asserts that the telephone will ring in about five minutes. The narrator is inclined to believe the TV representative in the end, thinking that the call will come from his wife on the other end of the telephone line for the last time, when their marital relationship has irreparably been damaged. But there is no objective basis for the validity of these statements and thought. His wife might arrive after all, or might not, as the representative tells him. The predicted telephone call involves at least three pairs of unresolved binaries with regard to its actualization and timing in addition to the caller's identity. Notwithstanding, he is convinced after all that his wife has abandoned him, albeit the notion is unfounded and forced on him.

A phone call possibly from a protagonist's absent wife who stays away at an unknown, unreachable location recalls an analogous situation with which *The Wind-Up Bird Chronicle* begins. Unlike the novel in which the protagonist has textual room of three volumes to strive for a reunion with his wife, psychical or otherwise, however, the short story's curtailed length likely indicates the termination of the relationship if the suffered damage is so considerable as the narrator is induced to believe, especially now that the narrator's very being as a human is in jeopardy. He holds no reason for hope to restore the tie with his missing wife in any of these cases.

In these two respects, there are a number of combined possibilities to occur after the ending, but none of them can claim undisputed legitimacy. The irresolution as a result of such entangled plotlines renders the ending into a kind of labyrinth, in which the reader hermeneutically gets lost. In fact, "TV People" finds itself congenial to magical realist works of such South American writers as Jorge Luis Borges (1899–1986), who penned short stories like "The Garden of Forking Paths" (1941) and "The Aleph" (1945), and Gabriel García Márquez (1927–2014), whose recently translated, yet unspecified long novel the narrator is reading. Murakami's text as a whole is similarly written somewhat like a maze, which one might enter lightheartedly as an uncomplicated reading game. The text hardly makes rational sense, however, and the reader can thus get metaphorically entrapped in the maze, since the game turns out much more serious and complex than it initially appears.

Murakami inserts the phrase, *osoroshii kaisen meiro* おそろしい回線迷路 (dreadful circuit maze) (*Zen sakuhin 1* [2002] 43), translated as "megacircuit" of the telephone line system (216), almost at the story's end, not only to hint at the impassability of almost infinite routes that disconnects the narrator from his wife[7] but also to finalize the text's labyrinthine quality and its implied literary affinity. This specific reference to a system that is too complicated to exit at the narrative's termination verifies not an open-ended development but the plot's ultimate breakdown.

Given the ending discussed above, a few questions arise as to what brings about the narrator's multifaceted demise, what attracts TV People as an instrument of the demise to him, and what the entire situation signifies beyond this particular case. In relation to the first two questions, a number of elements suggest what might be amiss with the way he lives. In a way, he appears to be no more than an ordinary resident of the city, just like the other narrator-protagonists discussed earlier. Beneath his appearance as a successfully married, regular office worker, however, lie some personal issues and idiosyncratic dissonance.

First, by principle, the narrator refuses to own or use certain mechanical amenities, such as TV sets and elevators, to the extent that his colleagues ridicule him as a modern-day Luddite. Obviously, his obdurate avoidance of the machinery, especially TV sets, largely accounts for TV People's strong interest in him. They do not have to approach the others, including his wife and colleagues, because TV has already appropriated them into its system. In other words, the humans, with a few exceptions, have thoroughly and willingly forfeited their position as thinking beings without resistance or questioning as far as their interaction with technology is concerned.[8] As such, they unreflectively behave as if a TV set or TV People did not exist, even when they are physically aware of the new device or intruding strangers close by. What TV people want is the conversion of a few resistant standouts. In this respect, the narrator is a social pariah, and the others treat him accordingly by refusing to discuss or acknowledge his conundrum over technology.

Second, apart from his aversion to technological assimilation, the narrator stays quite aloof of human connection and commitment in both public and private spheres, although he does not regard his detachedness as unusual. In his public role as an office worker for a major electronics company that rivals Sony, he works competently enough to be fairly well regarded by his department head. He self-admittedly does not feel, however, much enthusiasm or satisfaction with his job, which mostly consists of long, smoke-filled meetings for marketing new products. For instance, the day after TV People's first intrusion into his life, he speaks up only once in one of those meetings to ease his sense of duty for receiving a salary. To worsen the unfulfilling environment of drudgery, he has not developed a close relationship with his colleagues, including the department head, whose lightly physical, habitual touch of intended cordiality he innately detests. Exceptionally, the narrator goes out for a drink after work with a man of his age once in a while, but this supposedly friendly colleague tensely ignores and silently interrupts his confiding as soon as he timidly ventures to mention TV People. In short, as a member of the paid team organized to ensure and enhance corporate profitability, the narrator is not isolated in his workplace, but he does not really connect to anyone more than what his expected duty requires.

As far as we can surmise from the text, the narrator does not have much social association in his private life, either. Unlike his wife who goes out to see her friends from high school days over dinner on some weekends, he prefers to stay home by himself, indicating few friends, if any, with whom he can socialize away from work. His unsociability extends to the family circle. As is usually the case with Murakami's writings, fictional or otherwise, parents are disregarded and are irrelevant to the story. Also unmentioned, siblings probably do not exist or matter for the narrator. He does have some other relatives, but he has not seen, for about ten years, a cousin to whom he does not feel very close, and he intends to write to her a letter of no attendance in response to her wedding invitation. It is easily inferable that, with a mutual feeling, she has sent him the invitation merely out of the formality of familial obligation.

The situation is even more problematic with his marriage of four years to his wife, who should undoubtedly be his single, most important companion. She works for a minor publisher of a niche journal with small, yet devoted readership. Still at an early stage in their careers, they work hard for professional success and for enough income to afford a middle-class urban lifestyle, equipped with an apartment in a so-called *mansion* apartment building and a car. When they are very busy with their respective office work, they hardly talk to each other for three days on end. It is partly because of their tight, ill-matched schedules that the narrator is inclined to decline his cousin's wedding invitation in favor of a long-planned vacation with his wife in Okinawa. Insufficient communication and deficient partnership constitute a large part of this married life.

Fairly typical of many of today's marriages in which both spouses have a full-time office employment, their case does not deviate from the norm very much. What makes this marriage striking is the balance of power that plays out between the two involved. Neither of them dominates over the other, but the wife has imposed her will on the husband in certain respects from the beginning, including having made him quit smoking upon getting married. She does not compromise, either, with regard to the precise arrangement of home interior objects. The small apartment is cramped with her research materials as well as with his books and records, and she does not allow him to disturb in the slightest the way she has placed her belongings, including magazines on the sideboard and shared furnishings like the large clock. Lest he displease her with his careless handling, he patiently yields to her meticulous placement as a necessary condition for keeping their marriage untroubled and does not shift the position of any items in their residence, except for his own possessions.

Generally speaking, a spouse often caters to the partner's whim or demand in order to keep their relationship intact. And, on her part, this wife might as well have made a concession to accommodate her husband's idiosyncrasy for life without TV, although her interest as the editor of a magazine about natural food and organic farming has possibly contributed to the mutual agreement on a less artificial way of living. Still, her uncompromising insistence on placing almost everything indoor under her control is oppressive. As the narrator guesses, her minute attention to the domestic space must exhaust her mind with stress, which probably reflects an unsurfaced, yet persistent fear and insecurity verging on neurosis about negotiating unmalleable reality. With the aforementioned deficiency of communication and companionship taken into consideration, there emerges a possibility of her underlying dissatisfaction with her married life, from which she might wish to get away before the husband understands the cause.

At the same time, through his submission to her will, he might keep peace at home, but not necessarily in mind. In his own dwelling, his life is mentally compartmentalized, consisting of a larger area that he shares with his wife, and a much smaller one exclusively for his own use. Constant caution about casually touching and altering the configuration of nearby objects outside his own small domain renders him psychologically strained and claustrophobic as a result, even fairly paranoid, which might partially account for his fixation on heterogeneous intruders of a reduced size into his personal space. The spouses' mounting inner crises, combined yet mutually unacknowledged, likely have significantly been undermining their marital relationship for some time until it has reached a point of no return or reparation as the TV representative declares at the end.

Of the two spouses, TV People have already taken the wife into their machination, considering the fact that, despite her strong penchant for order, she, on her return home after their first intrusion, totally ignores the disorderly aftermath of what the technicians have done in the living room, including the newly installed, not preapproved TV set, her disarrayed magazines, and the clock displaced on the floor. Given no TV exposure at home, it is only inferable that her induction into their fold has taken place at her work or in the past before marriage when she probably used to watch TV. The narrator, on the other hand, remains an unfinished business for TV People, for he has adamantly lived his adult years without TV. And his case must intrigue them all the more for his deep occupational engagement in the proliferation of new TV products.

The story begins with TV People's covert, yet daring onset on him, because the time has finally ripened for their maneuver against this exceptional individual. The exact timing cannot be haphazard and unplanned, for the opening pages show the narrator in a very vulnerable state. Physically, he stays alone at home. Socially, as explained above, he is isolated. He also reveals his detachment from the traditional Japanese culture through his total disregard for sensitivity to nature and seasonal changes in his urban habitat. Spatially, he feels strained and ill at ease in his own private surroundings. And, temporally, he habitually finds himself vaguely anxious and disoriented at twilight on early Sunday evenings. The oxymoronic headache of a dull, yet piercing sensation is the first sign, accompanied by the hallucinatory perception of jarring noises, including the large clock's mechanical movement and a stranger's footsteps reverberating in the hall outside the apartment.

These two sensory phenomena are so certain to strike him on a weekly basis that he anticipates them at the specific time, almost like an obsession. The two kinds of noises, rather than being presented merely as playfully distorted, onomatopoeic transcriptions, refer to the relentless progression of time and tacit ostracism that the narrator cannot alter. One of them comes literally from a solid device for indicating time within the domestic walls where he feels constrained, while the other metaphorically stands for the society that alienates him externally. The narrator is so intimate with the noises that he has internalized them, promptly answering to the wife's question with a similarly dissonant, almost unpronounceable phrase, サリュッッップクルゥゥゥツ transcribed as "*SLUPPPKRRRZ*" (198) (*Zen sakuhin 1* [2002] 18), before realizing its nonsensicality and taking it back. The noises, as well as the headache, result from the persistent unease over lost time and opportunities in the form of a mounting list of the Sunday plans that he has failed to carry out. Coupled with the dreary prospect of a weekday labor cycle to begin just overnight, the noises and the headache beset the narrator with such intensity of discomfort that he lies stupefied, both mentally and physically, in the gathering dusk of his living room, exposing himself as a ready target before TV People's arrival.

Unrealistic and surreal as they are, TV People's properties can be understood in terms of Sigmund Freud's speculation on the uncanny, Jean Baudrillard's notion of simulation, and J. Hillis Miller's definition of the paranormal with support from Walter Benjamin's exposition on the technology of reproducibility. These theories interrelatedly work together effectively to explain Murakami's nonhuman beings. First, Freud's idea of the uncanny is relevant here more for what does not apply to Murakami's short story. The psychoanalyst classifies the uncanny phenomena into two kinds, one that we feel "when repressed infantile complexes have been revived," and the other "when the primitive beliefs we have surmounted seem once more to be confirmed" (Freud 157). The "castration-complex" (Freud 138), including the fear of such dismemberment as damage to eyes, typically exemplifies the first kind. This does not apply to Murakami's narrator-protagonist, because he is not concerned at all about a localized physical damage of that kind, repressed or not, to his body, and there is no single reference to the past of his childhood in which a repression must originate. A repressed trauma from the past does not lie within the scope of this story. The second group consists of the superstitious fear that the rational mind rejects, such as the revival of the deceased and human lookalikes coming to life. This is not the case with TV People, because they are neither revived dead beings nor animated dolls. Infused with aliveness, they act like humans.

Above all, in contrast to the Freudian uncanny that fills the subject with "dread and creeping horror" or "feelings of unpleasantness and repulsion"

(Freud 122, 123), TV People do not terrify or discomfort the narrator with a sense of repugnance at all. Still, the narrator intrinsically senses a muted sort of weird awkwardness that disquiets the mind in face of TV People. He tentatively calls the instinctive feeling "何かしら奇妙な印象 (an inexplicably strange impression)" or "居心地の悪さ (uncomfortableness)" (*Zen sakuhin 1* [2002] 16), ascribing it to the proportional reduction of their physical size.

In fact, Freud's etymological investigation into the term has certain bearings on the current case. Citing Schelling, he states that *unheimlich*, "literally 'unhomely'" in German and translated into English as *uncanny*, came to assume the same meaning with its presumed opposite, *heimlich*, as "something long known to us, once very familiar . . . that ought to have remained hidden and secret, and yet comes to light" (Freud 123–24, 124n, 130). The Freudian uncanny recurs through "the process of repression" (Freud 148). As discussed above, however, repression does not have a role in the narrator's psychology. Instead, the uncanny arises extrinsically in the form of TV People. They take advantage of his underlying susceptibilities to impose themselves upon him, because the medium they represent has been "long known" and "very familiar" to him in spite of his flat refusal to have it at home.

His affinity with TV partly comes from his office work in which he contributes to the further propagation of its influence. More importantly, like everyone else around him, he lives in the society that presupposes TV's presence as an integral part of its working, and he is exposed to its dominance whether he accepts it or not. He has become so familiarized with TV's presence as to internalize it. For instance, after coming back home from work and waiting for his wife's return, he fails to kill time effectively by deliberately reading the tedious newspaper more than once, and he cannot bring himself to write a letter, due now, of no wedding attendance to his cousin. The indeterminate suspense with little motivation is typical of what the social norm prescribes as a kind of time to be spent on watching TV aimlessly for the sheer sake of letting time pass. Old-fashioned means, such as reading a newspaper and writing a letter, which he tries, fail him. Without consciously realizing what he needs but lacks, he misses a regular, functional device to watch. There is no wonder, then, that he has felt strong fascination with the set from the beginning once TV People install it in his living room even though the machine does not show any recognizable content. The following evening, however, he cannot even manage to activate the TV, although he tries multiple times with a remote control, before it turns on by itself to show the TV representative on the screen.

Although unidentified as such, the representative first appears on the Sony color TV set that a team of three TV People carries around in the narrator's bleak dream of an office meeting. When he wakes up, the narrator finds the same image gazing at him from the living room TV. The correspondence between dream and reality suggests TV People's successful infiltration, like "夢の尻尾 [the tail of a dream]" (*Zen sakuhin 1* [2002] 38), not only into his physical private space but also into his subconscious. They are neither inhabitants of the dream sphere nor a projection of disturbed or repressed psychology upon reality. Instead, they "ought to have remained hidden and secret" behind the TV screen "and yet come to light" in daily life while getting discreetly internalized without resistance as "something . . . very familiar" and "long known" in the psychic space that they find congenial. This familiarity partly accounts for their unassertive kind of uncanniness.

TV People are unacknowlegedly familiar to the narrator, because they, as simulacra, embody the sort of life that he and the other members of society live. By calling them by the *katakana* transcription of the English word "ピープル (people)," which is highly unusual, if not impossible, in actual Japanese usage, he distinguishes them from humans from the very beginning. He thus considers these human lookalikes from the televisual sphere of artificial illusion alien, even somehow false in contrast to actual humans. But the real as genuine can no longer be validly discriminated from the imaginary as false, because simulation compromises the distinction between those binaries and brings forth amalgamated truth or reality as a result. As Baudrillard puts it regarding cartography, "it is the generation by models of a real without origin or reality: hyperreal," and TV, along with Disneyland, is the critic's favorite example of such "a hyperspace" in today's world. In other words, our epistemology faces "a question of substituting signs of the real for the real itself," which constitutes "an operation to deter every real process by its operational double" (Baudrillard 169–70). Emerging as human-like emissaries from the TV hyperspace to affect the external world, TV People function as a sign incarnate of "operational double."

Although TV People appear like humans, certain aspects of their behavior are more aligned with mechanical qualities, such as their singly focused, "効率よく (efficiently)" acted-out purposefulness, the representative's precisely regulated way of stepping down the stairs, and his paper-thin voice devoid of intonation (*Zen sakuhin 1* [2002] 22). This mechanical nature accounts for the second source of TV People's uncanny impression, not just because they are affiliated with a machine but also because, as agents of simulation, they operate to transmute the world into an extension of the televisual space. According to Baudrillard, simulation, by way of "any technical apparatus, which is always an apparatus of reproduction," constitutes "the place of a gigantic enterprise of manipulation, of control and of death," and he associates a resulting "anguish, a disquieting foreignness," and "uneasiness" with Benjamin's theory of the mirror image (Baudrillard 185; see also Benjamin 32–33).

Without transforming social reality, TV People manipulatively, yet unnoticeably approximate it to the TV hyperspace through simulative reduction, thereby achieving the effect of reproduction that manifestly begins with their shrunken physique. To the extent that it hardly brings about any caution or attention to humans, their size is reduced, because "genetic miniaturization is the dimension of simulation," and, theoretically, they "can be reproduced an indefinite number of times" (Baudrillard 170). Their reduced physical size not only defines their proper domain behind the small screen through which they emerge but also corresponds to the reductive way of thinking with which electronic media affect the viewer into accepting their information with little questioning. The process is well demonstrated toward the end of the story when the narrator initially objects to the TV representative about the shape of an object in the making at a factory environment on television. The large, black, strange machine on which the other two TV People are assiduously working looks like a "giant orange juicer" to him at first (213). As the unflustered representative who stands next to him talks to him as if coaxing a recalcitrant child, however, the narrator finds the representative's preposterous proposition of the object in question as an airplane growingly believable and finally irrefragable without being rationally convinced. In this mindset, the narrator also comes to accept the representative's assertion about his damaged married life and the wife's desertion without offering any voiced refutation.

The external reduction of the body turns out symptomatic of what undergoes inside mentally. As his intellectual capacity is reduced to merely repeating and thinking what the representative dictates to him, the narrator finds his palm apparently a little minified. Other symptoms of reduction include the awareness of his very existence as "とてもうすっぺら (very thin)," and his voice that increasingly loses depth and human expressiveness, becoming like the representative's as he converses with the nonhuman counterpart that watches over his transformation (*Zen sakuhin 1* [2002] 42).

In this way, TV People affect society to make it a copy of their own proper sphere without altering its manifest structure and detail. As a token of the simulatively copied world, the phonetically challenging, dissonant noises that the narrator hears in his living room the evening before, especially those of the large timepiece, prove not to be merely strange, isolated phenomena. Instead, they reveal themselves of the same nature with the mechanical noises of the huge machinery that the two factory workers are making. The two similar noises sound shortly one after another as if mutually responding from each side of the TV, while the narrator is losing humanity or facing imminent death. Those distorted noises he hears on early Sunday evenings, then, turn out to announce the opening of a passage from the world of televisual simulacra to the one being simulated, presaging indeed an arrival of intruders, at once familiar and yet unknown, accompanied by a muffled sensation of deep surgical penetration into the partially anesthetized brain, just like TV People's discreet way of infiltration into the psyche.

The two sides acoustically correspond to each other, because the TV screen no longer imperviously demarcates the presumably authentic, yet now compromised reality from televisual simulation. Not hermetically delimited any more, the TV sphere exudes through the osmotic screen to fully effect an unpronounced, fundamental change outside, in the form of TV People. In this sense, rather than being supernatural, their presence proves to be that of the paranormal in Miller's terminology:

> A thing in "para" is . . . not only simultaneously on both sides of the boundary . . . [but] also the boundary itself, the screen which is . . . a permeable membrane connecting inside and outside . . . dividing them but also forming an ambiguous transition between one and the other. (Miller 441)

As such, TV People traverse the TV screen from the electronic field to the tangible world of materials and vice versa without much difficulty. At the same time, the televisual space that appears three-dimensional in the apparatus behind the screen, in fact, presents itself on the screen's exposed surface two-dimensionally only when the device is in operation. In this sense, the very TV screen constitutes their presence, which explains why they never maneuver far away from a TV set as demonstrated first in the narrator's living room. As for his office, including the reproduced one in his dream, the entire corporate space is solely aimed at designing and marketing such consumer electronic devices as TV for maximal profits, enabling TV People to move around at ease, like the proverbial fish in water.

This paranormal nature thus prescribes their spatiotemporal presence. As the protagonist specifies at the beginning of his narration, it is the intermediary brief span of time, a temporal "permeable membrane connecting" day and night, when they first encroach on his living space. He is fully aware that, for their infiltration, they deliberately choose "時刻の薄闇 (the twilight of time)" on a Sunday evening when he habitually lies paralyzed and vulnerable (*Zen sakuhin 1* [2002] 16). On the solitary way to his office of the ninth floor the following Monday morning, he encounters the TV representative walking down the steps on "四階と五階の間の階段 (the stairs between 4th and 5th floors)" (*Zen sakuhin 1* [2002] 29). Deserted as a result of people's reliance on the elevator, the path of stairs as a place of spatially "ambiguous transition" between two populated floors is one variation of Murakami's loci where an unreal or extraordinary event takes place. A short story, "*Doko de are sore ga mitsukarisōna basho de* どこであれそれが見つかりそうな場所で (Wherever I'm likely to find it)" (2005), offers another instance. A resident and Merrill Lynch trader, who also avoids using the elevator, has apparently disappeared without a trace on the landing of stairs between twenty-fifth and twenty-sixth floors in his high-rise *mansion* building. In *1Q84*, the abandoned stairway off a congested highway that Aomame goes down in her unintentional passage into the simulative world with two moons, which she later terms 1Q84, is also a variation.

An intermediary space of paranormal nature is central to Murakami's fiction, as the character often seamlessly transitions through it from the world of his or her normalcy to another of a new dimension with varying degrees of unfamiliarity to them. In addition to the previous examples, one may mention *watashi*'s entry through a ladder into Tokyo's subterranean world where insidious creatures called Yamikuro lurk in *Hard-Boiled Wonderland and the End of the World* or, in *Killing Commendatore*, the narrating painter's descent into the other world of *metaphors* through a hole that suddenly opens up on the floor of an older painter's sickroom he is visiting.

The traversing is not one-directional, and not only human figures who, if fortunate, manage to come back after all but also many kinds of nonhumans make the transition. For instance, in Chapter 48 of *Kafka on the Shore*, an unidentified, slimy creature of malign nature "squirm[s] out of [dead] Nakata's mouth," before Hoshino succeeds in closing the opened path it seeks by turning a large, heavy stone.[9] Similarly, the "ominous"-sounding "Little People" come out of the open mouth of a sleeping ten-year-old girl who has been severely abused sexually to the detriment of her mental and reproductive faculties in Chapter 19 of *1Q84*.[10] In turn, in Chapter 21 of *Killing Commendatore*, the eponymous character comes alive as a self-proclaimed "Idea" in the form of a reduced copy of one of the figures on a recently discovered painting, while another character from the same painting, who identifies himself as "a Metaphor, nothing more," pops out of the hole in the room of that dying old man who painted it in Chapters 51 and 52 (*Killing Commendatore* [2018] 236, 550). Both the embodied "Idea" and "Metaphor" as well as the TV representative belong to the compressed, intermediary plane field of either a canvas or a TV screen, out of which they emerge.

The transitional space facilitates the traversing and lessens the expected impact of violation, which relates to the East/West difference that Murakami posits. The Western imagination sharply and inviolably separates this familiar world of the living from the other, unknown counterpart, and the crossing, if any, entails inevitable friction and a great sense of infringement. By contrast, Japan and East Asia show "a unique kind of pre-modernity" in which reality and unreality coexist side by side and "traversing the border this way or that is natural and smooth, depending on the situation" ("*Umibe no Kafuka*" [2003c] 13–14, 16, 38–39), as already mentioned in chapter 1. Murakami ascribes the unreal elements of his fiction in general to this traditional East

Asian sensitivity to traversable duality. Thus, a device that makes the passage hardly laborious and remarkable, if not quite "natural and smooth," functions in his literature as an intermediary space between two worlds.

Accordingly, even when one of the alien TV People comes out of the TV set, the action only requires on the representative's part the same amount of physical exertion as going through just a regular, somewhat narrow opening like a window, rather than forcibly trespassing upon another dimension. On his part, as if hypnotized, the narrator does not make any reaction or express any horror. It follows that Murakami here is interested in TV not necessarily as a piece of technology per se but as a pathway from another world, and TV People prove to be paranormal rather than supernatural by nature, being more "televisual virtual images" than "cyborgs, computer simulations or AI . . . creations" (Monnet 346). Thoroughly, yet slickly assimilated into the reality that TV as a dominant medium of information has at once saturated and simulated, their presence is already felt familiar even if one has not seen them materialized before. That sense of uncalled-for, unacknowledged familiarity causes the narrator an unaccountable uneasiness that verges on the uncanny.

What fundamentally renders them uncanny, however, is their ability to transfuse themselves into the human psyche, take over the mind, and dismantle the self in the process of making it a copy in their expanding hyperspace. At the end of the story, the self disintegrates as a result of media influences. The Western philosophical endeavor in the last four centuries has placed primal emphasis on the solidified consciousness of one's own interiority as irreplaceably unique, independently contained, and sharply contrasted to social exteriority as an individual entity. The construction of the self was posited as a project of central, and increasing importance since Descartes and the Enlightenment, culminating in its apparent actualization with modernity. Now, as Jameson notes as "one of the fashionable themes in contemporary theory," the "formerly centered subject or psyche" is considered *"decentering"* in postmodernity (Jameson 15; emphasis in the original).

This "disappearance of the individual subject" (Jameson 16), if fact, was happening as the sense of the self almost attained the status of a given while its basis was eroded through modernization, or more specifically, technological advance for reproducibility, the wide effects of which concern Walter Benjamin's tenet. His interest pertains to the greatly enhanced technology of reproduction in the early twentieth century and its profound implications on artistic practice and sociopolitical reality. He discusses the "authenticity" or the "aura" of an artifact as its "core," arguing that "the destruction" thereof "is the signature of a perception" that "by means of reproduction . . . extracts sameness even from what is unique" (Benjamin 22–24). Abundant copies that the technology of reproducibility made readily available began to cripple the artistic "authenticity" when most urban inhabitants already "relinquish[ed] their humanity in the face of an apparatus" (Benjamin 31). If we treat the self as an intellectual construct with "authenticity," the underlying analogy is obvious.

The constructed self was even more precarious in Japan's modernity that was hastily imported and implemented in a matter of half a century. Self was an ill-fit covering imposed on the Japanese psyche whose orientation was traditionally communal. The resulting conflict is evident, for instance, in *Kokoro* こゝろ (1914) by Natsume Sōseki, with the nation hovering on the threshold of full modernity at the end of the Meiji Period. Of particular interest in this context is *Tomodachi* 友達 (*Friends*) (1967) by Abe Kōbō, which came out more than two decades after World War II, when individualism supposedly took root on the adoptive soil. A nine-membered, three-generational family without kinship to the protagonist suddenly impose themselves on him and take over his private living space, claiming that the solitary figure needs their surrogate companionship. Incarcerated in his own apartment, he eventually dies as a result of the *comfort* they provide against his will. The play offers an ironic social commentary on the majority principle of the constitutionally implemented, postwar democratic regime.[11] More importantly, Abe exposes the fragile basis of individuality in mid-twentieth-century Japan, where the crafted selfhood still remained fragile and vulnerable to the binding force of a communal entity of the family.

In the next few decades, the unstable status of the self did not change, while the communal cohesion that once suppressed individualistic assertion diminished mainly through structural disintegration of the family system from multigenerational to nucleus, then often to even smaller social units. The comparison with Abe's *Friends* reveals that, by the time "TV People" was written, the individual has lost meaningful contact with the rest of society, including his own immediate relatives, along with the social restructuring. Without the familial bond that used to define and sustain a person's social identity, the self is left on its own. In lieu of a socioculturally hereditary system, what approaches and appropriates the now exposed, isolated, and not fully developed self is electronic media, more specifically TV in this case, that fill the widening relational gap among humans with a pervasively overflowing amount of information.

It follows that Murakami's short story illustrates the process of the dismantlement of the self as a construct of modernity. While the process involves some particularly Japanese elements, it basically applies to any place that is televisually affected. By definition, the self is supposed to have its solid agency, but its foundation actually does not stand very certain, while it remains unguardedly susceptible to influences from new inventions of telecommunication for simulative reproducibility. The ambiguous ending of "TV People," with external signs of two alternative outcomes for the protagonist—physical petrification or metamorphosis into a nonhuman form—alludes to what is happening internally. Not only is the self dismantled to the death of humanness, but it is also altered as one of the "depthless . . . postmodern subjectivities" that simulate the television system (Monnet 351). The human consciousness becomes another "permeable membrane" to allow and identify with televisual infusion. That is the ultimate source of the uncanny that the narrator feels upon encountering TV People as they paranormally infiltrate first through the TV screen, then further into the self, which they find readily transmutable to their simulative manipulation. In the end, the self simply copies what TV presents as the real.

As their identically copied appearance indicates, TV People's human-like form is a temporary result of the necessity to insert themselves into the physical world. Coming from the electronic field, they originate in the TV screen's "白い光、ノイズ (white light, noise)" out of which the representative emerges (*Zen sakuhin 1* [2002] 27). The televisual system seeks to place isolated individuals collectively under its control. As long as it achieves its aim, the content of broadcast information does not matter. The white noise,[12] therefore, stands for its ultimate form of enthrallment of human viewers, as that happens to the narrator as well. His initial interest in the new TV's blank screen lasts less than half a minute. Later in the middle of that night, he finds himself gazing at the white light with static noise for a longer time. Finally, the following evening, he gets frustrated with the TV, which fails to turn on in spite of his many attempts, to the extent that he misses the white noise, signaling his readiness for incorporation into the televisual system, just before the representative's embodied emergence.

Murakami leaves certain aspects of the story untold or unexplained. First, while TV People function as manifested agents of the TV system that encroaches on the human psyche, it is not mentioned who or what organization operates them at the center of the system. Second, it is also not clear at what point of time, in what situation, and for what reason the narrator tells his story to the reader. The first question pertains to many of Murakami's stories, as the preceding two chapters also illustrate. Indicative of the insidious nature of the postmodern society in which the center of power stays obscure and unidentifiable, those stories do not ascribe the source of manipulation to a single individual/organization or a cluster of them. Even when those entities are named, such as the star-marked sheep in *A Wild Sheep Chase*, the Calcutecs in *Hard-Boiled Wonderland and the End of the World*, and Wataya Noboru in *The Wind-Up Bird Chronicle*, among others, they are not presented as *the* villain(s) whose immediate removal alone would solve the problem. Instead, these elusive figures are always suggestive of the larger machination that stays behind and unspecifiable while infusing them with unmitigated, malevolent will to power,[13] with its effect going far beyond mere surveillance, as "TV People" illustrates.[14]

With regard to the second question, the protagonist's narration in past tenses in the original Japanese text places the story's formation after its ending. On the one hand, this makes it awkward for him to be telling his personal account after he has lost his existence as a human being. On the other hand, he offers a narrative of what has transpired to him without critiquing at all how adroitly TV People infringed on his life, which is compatible with his posthuman phase. These considerations altogether make it clear again that, while somewhat concerned about a larger aspect of postmodernity, this short story primarily focuses on the fundamental effect of electronic, televisual media on humanity in the reductive form of terminal functionaries. They are pervious not only to the TV screen but also to the human psyche, effectually transmuting and appropriating people's critical thinking, autonomous will, and emotions that should render them human. Without being didactic, Murakami writes a cautionary story about too much dependence on the television system. Three decades after the publication, however, the text increasingly seems to have foreshadowed the humanity's current situation in which pervasive electronic media of far more handy, powerful devices have profoundly been affecting us by providing all too ready access to the advanced/ advancing Internet.

In the last chapter that follows, we will further elucidate the nature of TV People by comparing Murakami's short story with a pair of horror movies in which a ghostly figure similarly emerges out of the TV screen.

NOTES

1. Four books came out respectively in 1998, 2000, 2001, and 2006 as a result of the first website correspondence between 1996 and 1999. The fifth book, *Shōnen Kafuka* 少年カフカ (*Kafka the Boy*) (2003), was based on correspondence from 2002 to 2003. Another book was issued in 2006 from the third online interaction early the same year. The latest book was published in July of 2015 in response to far more readers' input from January to May that year.

2. *Killing Commendatore* 262, 634. All the references to this novel are to its translation by Philip Gabriel and Ted Goossen in 2018.

3. Similarly, the protagonist of *Killing Commendatore* expresses his personal aversion about the idea of having an operation remotely conducted by a surgeon via the Internet (119), and a friend ridicules him for his out-of-date mindset (446).

4. Unless otherwise noted, all the references to the short story "TV People" are to its translation by Alfred Birnbaum in *The Elephant Vanishes* (1993).

5. *Murakami Haruki zen sakuhin 1990–2000 1* (2002) 294. See also *Mimizuku* (2017) 251–52.

6. *Murakami Haruki zen sakuhin 1990–2000 1* (2002) 40. All the references to this short story in the original are to this edition.

7. Again, *The Wind-Up Bird Chronicle* shows a similar situation in which its protagonist guesses the possible presence of his missing wife on the other end of the underground cable system. See its translation by Jay Rubin in 1997a, 485.

8. Kuritsubo (281) refers to this process succinctly.

9. *Kafka on the Shore*, trans. Philip Gabriel (2005a) 451–54.

10. *1Q84*, trans. Jay Rubin and Philip Gabriel (2011a) 240, 249–50. Unless otherwise noted, all the references to this novel are to this translation.

11. Kuritsubo (274–75, 284) discusses the same situation in Abe's short story, "*Chinnyūsha* 闖入者 (Intruders)" (1951), which is a prototypal text for the play, in terms of the majority principle and an individual's alienation.

12. This phrase recalls the postmodern novel by Don DeLillo, *White Noise* (1984).

13. What Ebisuno in *1Q84* states about Little People is suggestive in this context, because Little People approximate TV People in several respects. According to him, in place of George Orwell's Big Brother who as an easily detectable figure has "no longer any place . . . in this real world of ours" (236), the unidentifiable Little People have appeared.

14. In this sense, rather than such phrases as "colonized . . . reality," "imperialistic . . . visuality," and "dictatorship" that suggest a political source of power, Monnet's mention of "a totalitarian and oppressive, if diffused vision" seems more appropriate to "TV People" (Monnet 346, 348, 351, 353).

Chapter 7

Televisual Appropriation and Fear in "TV People" and *Ringu*

As we have seen in the previous chapter through a close examination of Murakami's "TV People" (1989), the televisual media has fundamentally affected human life for decades since the proliferation of TV, even before the arrival of the cyberspace. Given the gravity of the situation, it is meaningful to go back to the precise moment in recent history when TV thoroughly integrated itself into human life, because how we live our current life, with the ongoing advancement of digitized technology and communication, has evolved as an extension from that near past. This chapter further explores the nature of the contact between humans and electronic, televisual media, by way of comparing "TV People" with a pair of popular Japanese horror films, *Ringu* リング (Ring) (1998, 1999),[1] directed by Nakata Hideo 中田秀夫 (b. 1961), which came out at the same specific moment. Of particular interest here is the triple spatial dynamics that involves the televisual field proper to TV, the fictional plane inhabited by the character watching TV, and the space of the film spectator or the text reader outside the fictional plane, demonstrated by these artistic creations from Japan at the end of the twentieth century. Both the short story and the films feature agents of paranormal nature (in J. Hillis Miller's definition), offering intriguing points of convergence and difference.

"TV People" and *Ringu* share the same predigitized technological settings. For the subject matter, they both center on the analog, nonflat TV set that needs an antenna for its one-directional radio reception, with channel options severely limited in today's standard. In the case of *Ringu*, the setting is doubly outdated with the videocassette system that, combined with analog TV, plays a pivotal role and yet has long given place to more efficient, powerful forms of visual reproduction, when DVD that replaced it is becoming obsolescent. One basic question pertains to them, though: why, despite the same technological settings and a shared visual motif of a nonhuman figure coming out of TV, do *Ringu* the films remain globally recognizable through the horror they inspire, while "TV People" does not necessarily enjoy such reception for the very same reason?

Apart from the scenes in which a team of shrunken people carry around a TV set into the narrator's life, the most striking image in "TV People" takes place when one of them appears on TV, gradually grows larger, and finally comes out of the screen. This disorienting scene in particular recalls *Ringu* in which Sadako, the ghostly female figure, similarly pulls herself out of a TV frame on her trudging advance to the target. In the mid-twentieth century, the teenager's adoptive father, afraid of her fatal cursing power, threw her alive into a solitary, abandoned well to her slow, gruesome death, decades before she reemerges as part of a short, edited film on a videotape that surfaces in a rental villa complex, built on the old well. People who watch the VHS tape usually receive an immediate telephone call that announces their death to occur a week later. Then, seven days later as foretold, the ghost unfailingly visits them from a TV set, leaving traces of victims who appear unnaturally shocked to death one after another, as if struck by a pernicious, communicative disease. To transfer the curse and avoid death, the haunted individual must make a copy of the videotape and show its content to another person before one week expires.

Despite having analog TV technology and a visual motif in common, *Ringu* differs from the literary counterpart in two respects. First, the ghost needs the videotape to be passed around by others. By contrast, the short story's shrunken technicians do not rely on any devices or people for their actions of carrying a TV set and forcing it upon an unsuspecting, targeted individual, especially on someone like the narrator-protagonist, who does not want to own one. Second, the ghost does not fail to prey upon her intended victims, exactly one week after they view the video as announced via telephone. Meanwhile, unlike her, TV People impose themselves on the narrator-protagonist at any moment of their choice during his daily routine, without giving him any leeway, such as a prior notice, a grace period, and a way to get out of his tightening quandary. The difference comes from degrees of the nonhuman's involvement with the nontelevisual field. Since TV People as terminal functionaries of TV simulation have already appropriated the external world except for a few remaining, resisting individuals, nothing stands in the way of their action. By contrast, once outside the televisual space, the ghost Sadako by definition is an inherently alien, incompatible element. She needs to parasitize a carrier for her move, and her operation is subjected to many physical restrictions. Accordingly, she laboriously crawls out of TV for spatial infringement, while the TV person steps out of the electronic screen easily without much physical exertion, entailing no sense of violation.

To a large extent, with a videotape as a new prop for the conduit of spectral transmission, *Ringu* the films constitute a refurbished update of a traditional ghost story, with Sadako as "a prime example . . . of the Gothic ghost of a picture" as Jerrold E. Hogle puts it (Hogle 174). Typically, someone under predetermined circumstances, such as presence at a wrong location and time, comes into contact with a supernatural being, often to his/her great fright or even demise as a result. The ghastly visitation that befalls the viewer precisely one week after the videotape playing, for instance, shows a reinvented version of an inauspicious situation approximated to the strict video rental terms, reinforced here with a punctual phone call immediately after the viewing, of a period beyond which a certain penalty is imposed. Thus, *Ringu* as a good horror film is expected to stir up the visceral, existential fear, akin to an animal survival instinct, in the victim as well as in the actual film spectator for whom the victim functions vicariously. The fear arises from an ancient part of the psyche against the rationalizing superstratum that attempts to place it under control. The effect is straightforward. Her oneiric emergence deep from the dark underground well symbolically suggests her close affinity with the unconscious regarding the impulsive fear she causes. In this respect, it might be coincidentally relevant to note that the Japanese word for a well, *ido* 井戸, is pronounced the same as the Freudian *id* in the Japanese language's transliteration.

In sharp contrast, this standard model of a ghost story obviously does not apply to the literary text, for TV People do not horrify the protagonist in the slightest when they appear in the circumstances most familiar and ordinary to him, and he does not regard them as a threat to his being. He also receives a telephone call at the story's end. Unlike those fatal calls in *Ringu*, however, this call is of indeterminate nature as explained in the preceding chapter above, and it does not frighten the narrator. As Matsuoka Kazuko claims Murakami's text to be a new kind of ghost story (Matsuoka 285), if the term is to have some validity, we need to examine it with regard to the different kind of predicament and fear, or the apparent lack thereof, that it entails.

Apart from the intrusive nature of their visits, TV People remain discreetly inconspicuous in behavior and appearance, including the proportional reduction of their physique. Suggestive of a situation of gradual encroachment on an individual's private and public life with his or her full awareness, this alludes to the effect of unobtrusively ubiquitous electronic media, particularly TV in this case, on people's life. Willingly embracing media's spread everywhere around human activities, people unreservedly incorporate media influences for the sake of ease and comfort in acquiring information and entertainment. The televisual media are so well integrated into every aspect of the social fabric that they can even affect the people, like the narrator-protagonist, who elect not to possess a TV set at home. The narrator also cannot avoid contact with the device due to the nature of his occupation. As a result, people are reduced to automaton-like beings that accept media-fed information unreflectively, becoming short of intellectual depth and diversity and scarcely distinguishable in thought from TV People, as it happens to the narrator in the end. This almost willing surrender of intellectual integrity is designed not to evoke a strong fear that would jeopardize the process. The skilled TV People know how to behave, and the narrator-protagonist does not feel horrified at any moment.

This televisual appropriation of human interiority does not mean, however, that electronic media can mold people's thought without any resistance, indicated by the fact that the narrator-protagonist questions the intrusive nature of TV People's visits from the beginning, although he cannot halt their infiltration. Unlike other people around him, he senses their appearance, behavior, and presence as being amiss and somewhat alien. These different responses to the shrunken intruders' maneuver signify most people's thorough familiarity with electronic media to the point of unconditional, unquestioning submission, in contrast to a few others' attempt to keep a conscious distance, albeit to little avail. The story "TV People" thus implies a kind of uneasiness shared and vaguely felt, yet almost unrecognized by people who have undergone the "ubiquitous technological mediation" of "contemporary cultural life" (White 41; see also Yu 117). While immersing themselves in "the comforting banality of today's technology" that has become "perhaps too familiar" just as they desire (Phu 49), people might sense—however vaguely and slightly in the very regular way they spend their quotidian hours exposed to television—an unarticulated anxiety about the state in which they have forfeited their autonomy as thinking beings.

To discuss more in detail "TV People" and the *Ringu* films as different kinds of ghost stories, let us return to the initial question raised earlier: why do the films retain their lingering circulation on a global scale while, in spite of the avid readership of his novels in many parts of the world, Murakami's short story has stayed relatively obscure? Upon their release, the films gained popularity in Japan, the United States, and elsewhere because they struck the right chord of underlying fear in the viewer's mind to resonate on both sides of the Pacific and beyond in conjunction with the 1990s overflowing videocassette proliferation. If horror films "have always been credited with articulating the dominant fears and concerns of their respective periods" as Valerie Wee states (Wee 57–58), what is the essential nature of this fear in *Ringu*, if not simply about an archaically haunting ghost? Does the short story partake of that contemporary fear in spite of its apparent lack thereof? If that is the case, how does the text differentiate itself from the films? Finally, why did the works of two different artistic modes appear with the same motif of a disfigured humanlike figure coming out of TV in the last decade of the twentieth century, when the televisual system thoroughly infused society with its operation?

In both cases, a basic anxiety stems from the seemingly innocuous device of visual transmission that furnishes virtually every household. Placed at a room corner, the television, "which many people consider almost a friend," might as well operate as a monitor to watch over our private life and keep us vulnerable in "the ultimate act of technological betrayal" (Parris 5). Recent technological developments in certain Internet-connected TVs and other devices actually prove that such electronic surveillance is no longer a mere speculation but a likely reality. On a more fundamental level, whether TV transmits information digitally or analogically, and even if the TV is off, the constant presence of an unclosed electronic window can imperceptibly stir up, once the fleeting idea of such a possibility comes across the mind, an irrational, yet persistently unsettling sense that the device might be taking in every minute aspect of our life with an unintermittent, insentient, nonhuman gaze.

Furthermore, with overflowing, unstoppable televisual influx all around them, people might feel, without realizing or acknowledging it, even an invasive force coming from the TV screen. This unclaimed sensation over constant surveillance and informational aggression takes the anthropomorphic form of a ghost and shrunken TV People in the two pieces. They are *para*normal phenomena, rather than supernatural ones of an old type, according to Miller's definition as cited before, and the previous chapter has already explained the paranormal properties of TV People. In spite of her obviously ghostly origin, Sadako should also be considered paranormal, because the traversable screen constitutes her very presence, and, as such, she does not stay very far away from the TV screen, just like TV People.

It is important to notice here that the spatial scheme of the films and the story is not just dichotomically opposed between subject (videotape viewers, the narrator-protagonist) and object (the ghost, TV People) but structured threefold, implicitly involving the film spectators and the textual readers who stand outside the films and the text. A central issue concerns the visualized other that, originally confined within TV, moves out to take over the proximate space around the viewing fictional subject outside the screen as a newly acquired domain of its agency, then extending the effect of spatial appropriation to the further external sphere of the actual subject that watches the films or reads the text as consumable artifacts.

In *Ringu*, the uneasy feeling about TV's constant presence turns into a direct, unmitigated fear of an image that forcibly violates the border between electronic simulacrum and assumed reality. The frightening ghost that infringes on the field immediately external of TV and affects people to their demise embodies the unconsciously constant sense that a certain, perhaps malign influence emanates from the confines of television. The fear is shared almost universally as TV saturates societies. Unlike traditional ghost stories in which supernatural beings target a select, unlucky few at a fixed locale, *Ringu* reveals its postmodern contemporaneity. The horror films hint at an apocalyptic outcome of the pandemic that might affect the entire humanity through "a self-perpetuating chain" of metaphorical viral contagion of video copies uncontrollably multiplied "from an always already lost original" as Sadako becomes "a potentially *global* presence."[2] Thus, theoretically, anyone in the world can sense vulnerability as a potential target of her attack, which lays the foundation for *Ringu*'s worldwide reception, because people anywhere, fictional or otherwise, live cognizant of TV's excessive influence.

The intense fear induced by Sadako directly reaches the film spectators outside the fictional zone via the vicarious victims who inadvertently watch her video clip in the *Ringu* films. The ghost threatens to transgress by the sheer force of terror not only the spatial divide between TV and its exterior but also the one that separates the fictional plane from where the film spectators reside. The threat can be doubly effective when the spectators also watch the films on television, rather than in a theater. In a metaphorical sense, people's heavy dependence on the electronic media, which are the ghost's proper domain, enables her to roam across the threefold spatial dynamics until she finally imposes herself on the film spectators through terrorization. With *Ringu*, however, the actual spectators outside the unfolding movie can ultimately hold onto the practical assurance about the impenetrable double divide between the two sides of the TV screen as well as the fictional versus the actual. Thus, they can rationally discredit televisual trespassing and can choose to seek and consume at will a nightmarish vision of transgression in the contained realm of fiction for aesthetic pleasure and the release of suppressed fear. In other words, for all the intense fear that they undergo, the film spectators extrinsic to Nakata's films can rest assured of their integrity as humans.

Murakami's short story, in contrast, addresses the very covert way TV gradually transmutes the viewers' mind while they do not even think of the need to resist televisual encroachment, despite the underlying, unnoticed angst. Precisely because the story does not bring forth intense fear, the text of "TV People" does not force the readers to get sensitized to the conterminous divide between TV's contained sphere and fictional character's reality, rather leaving them in muffled confusion over the textual meaning of unreal occurrences placed in familiar settings. The bewilderment, in turn, helps to blur the demarcation between the textual plane and the readers' world, because their life's reality might unsuspectedly appear as a continuum of electronic media saturation from fictional representation. Murakami's intentionally easy reading style helps dilute further the supposedly inviolable boundary of fictionality and the readers' actuality. They thus get disarmed of apotropaic defensive rationalizing, unlike *Ringu*'s film spectators.

The paranormal TV People take over the adjacent space across a TV screen unassumingly, without giving a warning or telltale signs of emerging monstrosity to the readers or the narrator-protagonist. In the case of the narrator's workplace, the televisual field fills the entire office building, where meetings take place to discuss the design and marketing of a new TV model. As a result, he encounters one of them walking down the stairs. In this sense, "TV People" can be called a ghost story of a new kind specific to our contemporary reality. The unlikely spectral figures affect all the members of society, including those who wish to avert the general outcome, without causing a sense of fear or alarm either to the story's TV viewer or to the reader who is also exposed to TV's overreaching influence. A ghost story that leaves its readers baffled in this manner, rather than straightforwardly terrifying them, hardly qualifies as a good example in the old sense of the term. From another viewpoint, however, the text, which stays relatively unknown due to its failure to instill fear, paradoxically attains the status as a new kind of ghost story that accurately portrays today's reality fraught with unacknowledged, undeclared fear.

Ringu, the ghostly horror films, and "TV People" as an expression of Murakami's creative mind seem to negotiate totally different kinds of apprehension in accessing analog TV technology for remotely receiving visual information. In fact, originating in the identical situation of TV saturation as a socially coordinated reality in the last decade of the twentieth century, both pieces center on the nonhuman, televisual image that approaches and strikes the defenseless human viewers across the screen. The imagination results from the spatial reality of TV's vicinity that is already technologically compromised. The televisual, paranormal figures have metaphorically gained the ability to move around TV, even beyond the real/fictional divide, and affect humans on both sides of the demarcation at their will. Symptomatic of what undermines society, the two works address in tandem, yet in different modes, the same predicament that befell humanity at the end of the millennium.

A few decades since, the televisual appropriation of space has exponentially accelerated with the further proliferation of electronic screens, especially small, lightweight, portable ones for accessing the cyberspace that is at once eclipsing and absorbing the TV system in electronically transacting a vast amount of audiovisuals. In 1999, the same year when *Ringu 2* premiered, Kuritsubo Yoshiki already pointed out the "legally" established residence of nonintrusive, soft-trodden "Internet People" among humans in the footsteps of Murakami's TV People (Kuritsubo 284). And the ghost has inevitably found the Internet system much more congenial to her electronically viral transmission than the cumbersome physicality of videotapes, roaming the cyberspace in the film *Sadako 3D* 貞子3D (2012). The paranormal intruders might not advance far away from electronic screens, but there is little doubt that the ubiquitous accessibility to the World Wide Web via portable devices greatly facilitates their process of taking over the users' entire reality.

NOTES

1. I refer to the two immediately sequential movies by Nakata, *Ringu* (1998) and *Ringu 2* (1999), as *Ringu* for my argument, not considering other *Ringu*-related works.

2. Rojas 417, White 41, and Yu 115. See also Hogle 171 and Phu 45.

Afterword

In May 2019, I visited Mycenae, Greece, to see the famed archeological ruins associated with Agamemnon. When a multitude of other tourists were gone late in the afternoon, those hilltop ruins lay quietly under the mild sun, surrounded by olive groves and fields of wildflowers between two nearby mountains. Highly fascinating as the historical site was, I had another reason to come by bus all the way from Athens. It was to stay in a hotel called La Petite Planète where Murakami Haruki and his wife spent one night some thirty-five years earlier. The hotel is well known to some of his readers in Japan, because of the two pages he wrote about the enjoyable encounter he had with the hotel founder and owner.[1]

I also enjoyed talking to one of the manager's two daughters who now manages the hotel with her sister. The hotel has been renovated and enlarged since Murakami's visit. The evening was not so pitch-dark as he had described but, like him, I savored my stay in the Greek countryside after having spent days in the bustling city of millions. Unfortunately, according to the amiable manager, her father had passed away the previous year and was buried in the cemetery beside the two-kilometer road to the ruins.

Although Murakami's travel essay is very short, it does not fail to impress the reader with a rhetorical question he asks at the very end. Because the hotel owner, who had quit the Greek air force years before (being disgusted with the conflicts in Cyprus), appears to be exuberantly happy with his family back in his village, Murakami comments on his obvious joy of life, to which the Zorba-like man replies without a moment's hesitation: "Of course, I'm very, very happy." This prompts Murakami to wonder how many people in Japan could answer in the same manner. At that time, Japan was just entering a period of so-called bubble economy awash with money, but Murakami's musing is revealing not only because the question easily extends far beyond his native soil but also because it clearly indicates his deep-seated concern for contemporary humanity.

A month after my visit to Mycenae, on June 26, 2019, Murakami celebrated the fortieth anniversary of his writing debut with some of his musician friends, in a cozy, live concert-like gathering in Tokyo. His career as a professional writer has now stretched over four decades. In my view, a sense of basic humanism underlies his entire fiction and underscores his critical stance throughout these four decades, and that is essentially why I am interested in this novelist. On the other side of Murakami's problematization of contemporary life through unique artistic representation actually lies his humanistic concern about the precarious existential condition in which we have placed ourselves. Therefore, in the present monograph, I have tried to show that this humanistic concern has been central to Murakami's literary oeuvre from the very beginning of his literary career and equally runs through the early short stories that I have analyzed here in some detail.

The title of this monograph, *Murakami Haruki and His Early Work: The Loneliness of the Long-Distance Running Artist,* also reflects this long-term perspective. The subtitle aims at emulating the playful side of Murakami's writing. It is an obvious pun on Alan Sillitoe's collection of short stories, *The Loneliness of the Long-Distance Runner* (1960), but there are three main reasons for the word choice. First, running is a philosophy of life for Murakami who chooses to run for pleasure, discipline, and the enhancement of creativity as I explained in the foreword and chapter 3. Second, since the debut with his first novel four decades ago, his books have constantly been in circulation for *a long run.* Many of his novels, for instance, were best sellers upon publication and have continuously remained in print. In fact, when abroad, it is one of Murakami's joys to find his translated books on the shelves of bookstores, considering himself fortunate not to have them out of print. Although he was initially not well known in the better part of the 1980s, he has been popular at home and across the world in *the long run.*

In the third place, unlike the joy resulting from the act of translation as explained in chapter 3, Murakami admits to the long-term solitary struggle and rigor that he has to sustain in writing a long fictional work. He can obviously rely on auxiliary support for a long writing project. He has been happily married to his wife for almost five decades. He has many friends. Still, the author fundamentally has to endure the arduous task of creating a novel all alone, for months or even years. More to the point, however, similar to Sillitoe and the other Angry Young Men of a few generations earlier, Murakami has maintained persistent distrust of the post–World War II sociopolitical system throughout his writing career, in a quiet sort of rage. Consequently, despite his popular success, Murakami has also experienced the *loneliness* that sets him apart from the contemporary Japanese literary and critical establishment and the Japanese writers who may aspire to become consecrated in their national literary canon, as discussed in chapters 1 and 2 of this monograph.

The main title, on the other hand, is self-evident, since chapters 4, 5, and 6 discuss three of his early short stories that I consider pivotal in the early stages of his writing career: "The Second Bakery Attack," "The Elephant Vanishes," and "TV People." The chapter arrangement reflects not only the order of publication dates but also certain shifts that took place in them. The basic framework remains the same, with a male narrator who is an office worker in his late twenties or early thirties living in a consumer society of urban settings. Still, apart from the subject matters, the textual perspective subtly changes through the stories in terms of the widening scope of problematization. Although not autobiographical, "The Second Bakery Attack" obliquely, yet specifically, refers back to the compromised political activism of Murakami's generation in their college days. "The Elephant Vanishes" more broadly navigates issues lurking in ordinary middle-class suburbia that the disappearance of an elephant foregrounds. Finally, "TV People" targets the effects of ubiquitous electronic media devices on humanity in general. This shift in critical scope, I have suggested, largely parallels a similar change that has taken place in Murakami's novels.

To present a more comprehensive picture of Murakami's writing as a whole, it would be necessary to delve closely into his other kinds of writing, especially novels that he deems central to his self-identity as a literary artist. Except for a few cases, all his novels are set in Japan, and the underlying antipathy against the system of power remains potent. His early novels have the same techniques and topical framework in common with the short stories. Meanwhile, his later novels show certain differences as a result of his attempts at new narratological devices, such as various voices and multiple perspectives, third-person narration, and more realistic techniques. Fundamentally, through particularities of the Japanese settings, his later novels tend to negotiate problems shared by many people regardless of nationality or cultural orientation, while the earlier novels tended to be still tied to his young day experiences. This change is what I have observed more succinctly in the three short stories I have examined. A full critical treatment would involve a long-distance running project, so to speak, of which the present monograph constitutes only the initial sprint. Meanwhile, I hope to have demonstrated that Murakami's short stories deserve closer critical attention than they have so far been accorded in relation to his literary oeuvre as a whole.

NOTE

1. *Murakami asahi-dō* (1984) 152–53. The short piece is titled "*Mikēne no shōwakusei hoteru* ミケーネの小惑星ホテル (The Little Planet Hotel in Mycenae)."

Appendix
Works by Murakami Haruki

NOVELS

Kaze no uta wo kike 風の歌を聴け (*Hear the Wind Sing*). Kōdansha 講談社, 1979.
1973 nen no pinbōru １９７３年のピンボール (*Pinball, 1973*). Kōdansha, 1980.
Hitsuji wo meguru bōken 羊をめぐる冒険 (*A Wild Sheep Chase*). Kōdansha, 1982.
Sekai no owari to hādoboirudo wandārando 世界の終りとハードボイルド・ワンダーランド (*Hard-Boiled Wonderland and the End of the World*). Shinchōsha 新潮社, 1985.
Noruwei no mori ノルウェイの森 (*Norwegian Wood*). Kōdansha, 1987.
Dansu Dansu Dansu ダンス・ダンス・ダンス (*Dance Dance Dance*). Kōdansha, 1988.
Kokkyō no minami, taiyō no nishi 国境の南、太陽の西 (*South of the Border, West of the Sun*). Kōdansha, 1992.
Nejimaki-dori kuronikuru: daiichi-bu, dorobō kasasagi hen ねじまき鳥クロニカル：第１部、泥棒かささぎ編 (*The Wind-Up Bird Chronicle: Part 1, The Thieving Magpie*). Shinchōsha, 1994.
Nejimaki-dori kuronikuru: daini-bu, yogen suru tori hen ねじまき鳥クロニカル：第２部、予言する鳥編 (*The Wind-Up Bird Chronicle: Part 2, The Prophesying Bird*). Shinchōsha, 1994.
Nejimaki-dori kuronikuru: daisan-bu, torisashi otoko hen ねじまき鳥クロニカル：第3部、鳥刺し男編 (*The Wind-Up Bird Chronicle: Part 3, The Bird-Piercing Man*). Shinchōsha, 1995.
Supūtoniku no koibito スプートニクの恋人 (*Sputnik Sweetheart*). Kōdansha, 1999.
Umibe no Kafuka 海辺のカフカ (*Kafka on the Shore*). Shinchōsha, 2002.
Afutā dāku アフターダーク (*After Dark*). Kōdansha, 2004.
Ichi-kyū-hachi-yon: bukku wan <shi-gatsu—roku-gatsu> 1Q84: Book 1 <4月――6月> (*1Q84: Book 1 <April—June>*). Shinchōsha, 2009.
Ichi-kyū-hachi-yon: bukku tsū <shichi-gatsu—ku-gatsu> 1Q84: Book 2 <7月――9月> (*1Q84: Book 2 <June—September>*). Shinchōsha, 2009.

Ichi-kyū-hachi-yon: bukku surī <jū-gatsu—jūni-gatsu> 1Q84: Book 3 ＜10月――12月＞ (*1Q84: Book 3 <October—December>*). Shinchōsha, 2010.
Shikisai wo motanai Tazaki Tsukuru to, kare no junrei no toshi 色彩を持たない多崎つくると、彼の巡礼の年 (*Colorless Tazaki Tsukuru and His Years of Pilgrimage*). Bungei shunjū 文藝春秋, 2013.
Kishidanchō goroshi: daiichi-bu, arawareru idea hen 騎士団長殺し：第1部、顕れるイデア編 (*Killing Commendatore: Part 1, The Emerging Idea*). Shinchōsha, 2017.
Kishidanchō goroshi: daini-bu, utsurou metafā hen 騎士団長殺し：第2部、遷ろうメタファー編 (*Killing Commendatore: Part 2, The Shifting Metaphor*). Shinchōsha, 2017.

SHORT STORIES

Chūgoku iki no surō bōto 中国行きのスロウ・ボート (*A Slow Boat to China*). Chūō kōron sha 中央公論社, 1983. Containing "A Slow Boat to China" (1980), "*Binbō na obasan no hanashi* 貧乏な叔母さんの話 (A Story about a Poor Aunt)" (1980), "*Nyūyōku tankō no higeki* ニューヨーク炭鉱の悲劇 (The Tragedy at a New York Coal Mine)" (1981), "*Kangarū tsūshin* カンガルー通信 (The Kangaroo Communiqué)" (1981), "*Gogo no saigo no shibafu* 午後の最後の芝生 (The Last Lawn of the Afternoon)" (1982), "*Tsuchi no naka no kanojo no chiisana inu* 土の中の彼女の小さな犬 (Her Little Dog in the Soil)" (1982), and "*Shidonī no gurīn sutorīto* シドニーのグリーン・ストリート (Green Street in Sydney)" (1982).
Kangarū biyori カンガルー日和 (*The Fair Kangaroo Weather*). Illustrations by Sasaki Maki 佐々木マキ. Heibonsha 平凡社, 1983. Containing "The Fair Kangaroo Weather," "*Shigatsu no aru hareta asa ni hyaku pāsento no onna no ko ni deau koto ni tsuite* 4月のある晴れた朝に100パーセントの女の子に出会うことについて (On Seeing My 100% Girl One Fine April Morning)," "*Nemui* 眠い (Sleepy)," "*Takushī ni notta kyūketsuki* タクシーに乗った吸血鬼 (A Vampire on the Taxi)," "*Kanojo no machi to, kanojo no men'yō* 彼女の町と、彼女の緬羊 (Her Town, and Her Sheep)," "*Bāto Bakarakku wa osuki?* バート・バカラックはお好き？ (Do You Like Burt Bacharach?)," "*Ashika matsuri* あしか祭り (The Sea Lion Festival)," "*Kagami* 鏡 (The Mirror)," "*1963/1982-nen no Ipanema musume* 1963/1982年のイパネマ娘 (The Ipanema Girl in 1963/1982)," "*Gogatsu no kaigansen* 5月の海岸線 (The Shoreline in May)," "*Dame ni natta ōkoku* 駄目になった王国 (A Ruined Kingdom)," "*Sanjū-ni-sai no deitorippā* 32歳のデイトリッパー (A 32-Year-Old Daytripper)," "*Tongari-yaki no seisui* とんがり焼きの盛衰 (The Rise and Fall of Tongari-Yaki)," "*Chīzu kēki no yōna katachi wo shita boku no binbō* チーズ・ケーキのような形をした僕の貧乏 (My Poverty in a Shape Like Cheese Cake)," "*Supagettī no toshi ni* スパゲティーの年に (In the Year of Spaghetti)," "*Kaitsuburi* かいつぶり (A Grebe)," "*Sausubei sutoratto* サウスベイ・ストラット (South Bay Strut)," and "*Toshokan kitan* 図書館奇譚 (A Strange Story of the Library)." Originally published in *Torefuru* トレフル, April 1981 to March 1983.

Hotaru, naya wo yaku, sono ta no tanpen 螢・納屋を焼く・その他の短編 (*Fireflies, Barn Burning, and Other Short Stories*). Shinchōsha, 1984. Containing "Fireflies" (1983), "Barn Burning" (1983), "*Odoru kobito* 踊る小人 (The Dancing Dwarf)" (1984), "*Mekura yanagi to nemuru onna* めくらやなぎと眠る女 (The Blind Willow and a Sleeping Woman)" (1983), and "*Mittsu no Doitsu gensō* 三つのドイツ幻想 (Three German Fantasies)" (1984).

Kaiten mokuba no deddo hīto 回転木馬のデッド・ヒート (*The Dead Heat of a Merry-Go-Round*). Kōdansha, 1985. Containing "*Rēdāhōzen* レーダーホーゼン (Lederhosen)" (1985), "*Takushī ni notta otoko* タクシーに乗った男 (The Man on a Taxi)" (1984), "*Pūrusaido* プールサイド (Poolside)" (1983), "*Ima wa naki ōjo no tame no* 今は亡き王女のための (For a Deceased Princess)" (1984), "*Ōto 1979* 嘔吐1979 (Throwing Up 1979)" (1984), "*Amayadori* 雨やどり (Taking Shelter from Rain)" (1983), "*Yakyūjō* 野球場 (A Baseball Field)" (1984), and "*Hantingu naifu* ハンティング・ナイフ (The Hunting Knife)" (1984).

Pan'ya saishūgeki パン屋再襲撃 (*The Second Bakery Attack*). Bungei shunjū, 1986. Containing "The Second Bakery Attach" (1985), "*Zō no shōmetsu* 象の消滅 (The Elephant Vanishes)" (1985), "*Famirī afea* ファミリー・アフェア (A Family Affair)" (1985), "*Futago to shizunda tairiku* 双子と沈んだ大陸 (Twins and the Sunken Continent)" (1985), "*Rōma teikoku no hōkai, 1881-nen no Indian hōki, Hittorā no Pōrando shinnyū, soshite kyōfū sekai* ローマ帝国の崩壊・一八八一年のインディアン蜂起・ヒットラーのポーランド侵入・そして強風世界 (The Fall of the Roman Empire, The 1881 Indian Uprising, Hitler's Invasion of Poland, and the World of Strong Winds)" (1986), and "*Nejimaki-dori to kayōbi no onna-tachi* ねじまき鳥と火曜日の女たち (The Wind-Up Bird and Tuesday's Women)" (1986).

TV pīpuru TVピープル (*TV People*). Bungei shunjū, 1990. Containing "TV People" (originally titled "*TV pīpuru no gyakushū* TVピープルの逆襲 (TV People Strike Back)" (1989), "*Hikōki: aruiwa kare wa ikani shite shi wo yomu yōni hitorigoto wo itta ka* 飛行機――あるいは彼はいかにして詩を読むようにひとりごとを言ったか (The Airplane: Or How He Talked to Himself As If Reading Poetry)" (1989), "*Warera no jidai no fōkuroa: kōdo shihon shugi zenshi* 我らの時代のフォークロア――高度資本主義前史 (The Folklore of Our Age: The Pre-History of Advanced Capitalism)" (1989), "*Kanō Kureta* 加納クレタ (Creta Kano)" (1990), "*Zonbi* ゾンビ (Zombi)" (1990), and "*Nemuri* 眠り (Sleep)" (1989).

"*Ao ga kieru* (Losing Blue) 青が消える (Losing Blue) (Blue Disappears)." 1992. In *Murakami Haruki zen sakuhin 1990–2000 1*, 273–82.

Rekishinton no yūrei レキシントンの幽霊 (*Ghosts in Lexington*). Bungei shunjū, 1996. Containing "Ghosts in Lexington" (1996), "*Midori-iro no kemono* 緑色の獣 (The Green Beast)" (1991), "*Chinmoku* 沈黙 (Silence)" (1991), "*Koori otoko* 氷男 (The Ice Man)" (1991), "*Tonī Takitani* トニー滝谷 (Tony Takitani)" (the long version in 1991; an original short version in 1990), "*Nana-banme no otoko* 7番目の男 (The 7th Man)" (1996), and "*Mekura yanagi to, nemuru onna* めくらやなぎと、眠る女 (The Blind Willow, and a Sleeping Woman)" (1995; a rewritten version of the 1983 story).

Kami no kodomo-tachi wa mina odoru 神の子どもたちはみな踊る (*All God's Children Dance*). Shinchōsha, 2000. Containing "*Yū ef ō ga Kushiro ni oriru* UFO が釧路に降りる (A UFO Descends on Kushiro)" (1999), "*Airon no aru fūkei* アイロンのある風景 (The Scene with an Iron)" (1999), "All God's Children Dance" (1999), "*Tairando* タイランド (Thailand)" (1999), "*Kaeru-kun, Tokyo wo sukuu* かえるくん、東京を救う (The Frog Saves Tokyo)" (1999), and "*Hachimitsu pai* 蜂蜜パイ (Honey Pie)" (2000).

Tokyo kitan shū 東京奇譚集 (*Strange Tales of Tokyo*). Shinchōsha, 2005. Containing "*Gūzen no tabibito* 偶然の旅人 (Accidental Traveler)" (2005), "*Hanarei bei* ハナレイ・ベイ (Hanalei Bay)" (2005), "*Doko de are sore ga mitsukarisōna basho de* どこであれそれが見つかりそうな場所で (Wherever I'm likely to find it)" (2005), "*Hibi idō suru jinzō no katachi wo shita ishi* 日々移動する腎臓のかたちをした石 (The Kidney-Shaped Stone That Moves Every Day)" (2005), and "*Shinagawa zaru* 品川猿 (A Shinagawa Monkey)" (2005).

Onna no inai otoko-tachi 女のいない男たち (*Men without Women*). Bungei shunjū, 2014. Containing "*Doraibu mai cā* ドライヴ・マイ・カー (Drive My Car)" (2013), "*Iesutadei* イエスタデイ (Yesterday)" (2014), "*Dokuritsu kikan* 独立器官 (An Independent Organ)" (2014), "*She'erazādo* シェエラザード (Scheherazade)" (2014), "*Kino* 木野 (Kino)" (2014), and "Men without Women" (2014).

Ichininshō tansū 一人称単数 (*The First Person Singular*). Bungei shunjū, 2020. Containing "*Ishi no makura ni* 石のまくらに (On the Stone Pillow)" (2018), "*Kurīmu* クリーム (Cream)" (2018), "*Chārī Pākā pureizu Bosanova* チャーリー・パーカー・プレイズ・ボサノヴァ (Charlie Parker Plays Bossa Nova)" (2018), "*Wuiz za Bītoruzu* With the Beatles ウィズ・ザ・ビートルズ" (2019), "*Yakuruto Suwarōzu shishū*「ヤクルト・スワローズ詩集」(The Collected Poems on the Yakult Swallows)" (2019), "*Shanikusai* 謝肉祭 (Carnaval) (Carnival)" (2019), "*Shinagawa zaru no kokuhaku* 品川猿の告白 (The Confession of the Shinagawa Monkey)" (2020), and "*Ichininshō tansū*" (2020).

SHORT SHORTS AND PALINDROMES

Yume de aimashō 夢で会いましょう (*Let's Meet in Dreams*). Cowritten with Itoi Shigesato 糸井重里. Tōjusha 冬樹社, 1981.

Zō kōjō no happī endo 象工場のハッピーエンド (*The Happy End of an Elephant Factory*). Illustrations by Anzai Mizumaru 安西水丸. CBS Sony, 1983.

Murakami asahi-dō chō tanpen shōsetsu: yoru no kumozaru 村上朝日堂超短編小説 夜のくもざる (*The Murakami Asahi Hall Super-Short Stories: Spider Monkeys at Night*). Illustrations by Anzai Mizumaru. Heibonsha, 1995.

Matatabi abita Tama またたび浴びたタマ (*Tama Showered with Silver Vine*). Illustrations by Tomozawa Mimiyo 友沢ミミヨ. Bungei shunjū, 2000.

Murakami karuta: usagi oishī Furansu-jin 村上かるた うさぎおいしーフランス人 (*Murakami Alphabetical Cards: The French Who Chased the Rabbit [and Found It Tasty]*). Illustrations by Anzai Mizumaru. Bungei shunjū, 2007.

ESSAYS, TRAVEL JOURNALS, AND AN AUTOBIOGRAPHY

Murakami asahi-dō 村上朝日堂 (*The Murakami Asahi Hall*). Illustrations by Anzai Mizumaru. Wakabayashi Shuppan Kikaku 若林出版企画, 1984.

Murakami asahi-dō no gyakushū 村上朝日堂の逆襲 (*The Murakami Asahi Hall Strikes Back*). Illustrations by Anzai Mizumaru. Asahi shinbun sha 朝日新聞社, 1986.

Rangeruhansu-tō no gogo ランゲルハンス島の午後 (*An Afternoon on the Islands of Langerhans*). Illustrations by Anzai Mizumaru. Kōbunsha 光文社, 1986.

"The Scrap": natsukashi no sen-kyūhyaku-hachijū-nendai "The Scrap" 懐かしの一九八〇年代 (*"The Scrap": The 1980s in Sweet Memories*). Bungei shunjū, 1987.

Hi izuru kuni no kōjō 日出る国の工場 (*Factories in the Country of the Rising Sun*). Illustrations by Anzai Mizumaru. Heibonsha, 1987.

Za sukotto fittsujerarudo bukku ザ・スコット・フィッツジェラルド・ブック (*The Scott Fitzgerald Book*). TBS Britannica ティービーエス・ブリタニカ, 1988.

Murakami asahi-dō haihō! 村上朝日堂 はいほー！ (*The Murakami Asahi Hall Hi Ho!*). Bunka shuppan kyoku 文化出版局, 1989.

Tōi taiko 遠い太鼓 (*A Drum Far Away*). Kōdansha, 1990.

Uten enten: Girisha, Toruko henkyō kikō 雨天炎天 ギリシャ・トルコ辺境紀行 (*The Rainy Weather, the Sweltering Weather: The Travel Journals of Remote Regions in Greece and Turkey*). Shinchōsha, 1990.

Yagate kanashiki gaikokugo やがて哀しき外国語 (*The Foreign Language That Makes Us Sad Before Long*). Kōdansha, 1994.

Murakami asahi-dō jānaru: Uzumaki neko no mitsukekata 村上朝日堂ジャーナル うずまき猫のみつけかた (*The Murakami Asahi Hall Journal: How to Find a Whirlpool Cat*). Illustrations by Anzai Mizumaru. Photographs by Murakami Yoko 村上陽子. Shinchōsha, 1996.

Murakami asahi-dō wa ikani shite kitaerareta ka 村上朝日堂はいかにして鍛えられたか (*How the Murakami Asahi Hall Has Been Trained*). Illustrations by Anzai Mizumaru. Asahi shinbun sha, 1997.

Henkyō, kinkyō 辺境・近境 (*Remote Regions, Nearby Regions*). Shinchōsha, 1998.

Fuwa fuwa ふわふわ (*Fluffy*). Illustrations by Anzai Mizumaru. Kōdansha, 1998.

Tsukaimichi no nai fūkei 使いみちのない風景 (*Scenes of No Use*). Photographs by Inakoshi Kōichi 稲越功一. Asahi shinbun sha, 1994. A paperback version with two more essays, Chūō kōron shinsha 中央公論新社, 1998.

Moshi bokura no kotoba ga uisukī de atta nara もし僕らのことばがウィスキーであったなら (*If Our Words Were Whisky*). Photographs by Murakami Yoko. Heibonsha, 1999.

Shidonī! シドニー！ (*Sydney!*). 2 vols. Bungei shunjū, 2001.

Murakami rajio 村上ラヂオ (*Murakami Radio*). Illustrations by Ōhashi Ayumi 大橋歩. Magajin hausu マガジンハウス, 2001.

Pōtoreito in jazu ポートレイト・イン・ジャズ (*Portraits in Jazz*). Illustrations by Wada Makoto 和田誠. Shinchōsha, 2004.

Hashiru koto ni tsuite kataru tokini boku no kataru koto 走ることについて語るときに僕の語ること (*What I Talk about When I Talk about Running*). Bungei shunjū, 2007.

Imi ga nakereba suingu wa nai 意味がなければスイングはない (*No Swing Without a Meaning* [*It Don't Mean a Thing if It Ain't Got That Swing*]). Bungei shunjū, 2005.

Zatsubun shū 雑文集 (*Collected Miscellaneous Writings*). Shinchōsha, 2011.

Ōkina kabu, muzukashii abokado: Murakami rajio 2 おおきなかぶ、むずかしいアボカド 村上ラヂオ 2 (*A Large Turnip, a Difficult Avocado: Murakami Radio 2*). Illustrations by Ōhashi Ayumi. Magajin hausu, 2011.

Sarada zuki no raion: Murakami rajio 3 サラダ好きのライオン 村上ラヂオ 3 (*A Lion That Likes Salad: Murakami Radio 3*). Illustrations by Ōhashi Ayumi. Magajin hausu, 2012.

"*Atsugi kara no nagai michinori: Ozawa Seiji ga Ōnishi Junko to kyōen shita 'Rapusodī in Burū': Saitō kinen fesutivaru Matsumoto gigu nisen-jū-san-nen kugatsu muika* 厚木からの長い道のり―小澤征爾が大西順子と共演した「ラプソディー・イン・ブルー」サイトウ・キネン・フェスティバル松本 Gig 2013年9月6日 (*The Long Distance from Atsugi: 'Rhapsody in Blue' that Ozawa Seiji Played with Ōnishi Junko: Saitō Commemorative Festival Matsumoto Gig September 6, 2013*)." *Kangaeru hito* 考える人 46 (Autumn 2013): 257–71.

Raosu ni ittai nani ga aru to yūn desu ka? Kikōbun-shū ラオスにいったい何があるというんですか？ 紀行文集 (*What on Earth Is There to See in Laos? Travel Journals*). Bungei shunjū, 2015.

"*Neko wo suteru: chichioya ni tsuite kataru tokini boku no kataru koto* 猫を棄てる―父親について語るときに僕の語ること (*Abandoning a Cat: What I Talk about When I Talk about My Father*)." *Bungei shunjū* 97, no. 6 (June 2019): 240–67.

Neko wo suteru: chichioya ni tsuite kataru toki 猫を棄てる―父親について語るとき (*Abandoning a Cat: When I Talk about My Father*). Bungei shunjū, 2020.

Murakami T: boku no aishita T-shatsu tachi 村上T 僕の愛したTシャツたち (*Murakami T: The T-shirts I loved*). Magajin hausu, 2020.

DIALOGUES AND INTERVIEWS

"*R. Chandorā aruiwa toshi shōsetsu ni tsuite* R・チャンドラーあるいは都市小説について (*On R. Chandler or the City Novel*)." In *Toshi no fūkei-gaku* 都市の風景学 (*Studies of Urban Scenery*), edited by Kawamoto Saburō 川本三郎, 6–59. Shinshindo shuppan 駸々堂出版, 1985.

Murakami Haruki, Kawai Hayao ni aini iku 村上春樹、河合隼雄に会いにいく (*Murakami Haruki Going to See Kawai Hayao*). Iwanami shoten 岩波書店, 1996.

Andāguraundo アンダーグラウンド (*Underground*). Kōdansha, 1997.

"Author Interviews: Haruki Murakami." Interview by Laura Miller and Don George. Salon.com. December 16, 1997. Accessed December 10, 2014. http://www.salon.com/1997/12/16/int_2/.

Yakusoku sareta basho de: andāguraundo 2 約束された場所で: *underground 2 (In the Promised Place: Underground 2)*. Bungei shunjū, 1998.

"*Murakami Haruki rongu intabyū: Umibe no Kafuka wo kataru* 村上春樹ロング・インタビュー:『海辺のカフカ』を語る (A Long Interview with Murakami Haruki: Talking about *Kafka on the Shore*)." Interview by Yukawa Yutaka 湯川豊 and Koyama Tetsurō 小山鉄郎. *Bungakukai* 文學界 57, no. 4 (April 2003): 10–42.

"*Haruki Murakami: écrire, c'est comme rêver éveillé.*" Interview by Minh Tran Huy. *Magazine Littéraire* 421 (June 2003): 96–102.

"Haruki Murakami: The Art of Fiction CLXXXII." Interview by John Wray. *The Paris Review* 170 (2004): 115–51.

"*Murakami Haruki rongu intabyū: Afutā Dāku wo megutte* 村上春樹ロング・インタビュー——『アフターダーク』をめぐって (A Long Interview with Murakami Haruki: Concerning *After Dark*)." Interview by the Editing Office. *Bungakukai* 59, no. 4 (April 2005): 172–93.

"'In Dreams Begins Responsibility': An Interview with Haruki Murakami." Interview by Jonathan Ellis and Mitoko Hirabayashi. *The Georgia Review* 59, no. 3 (Fall 2005): 548–67.

"Sean Wilsey Talks with Haruki Murakami." In *The Believer Book of Writers Talking to Writers*, edited by Vendela Vida, 241–50. San Francisco: Believer Books, 2005.

"Look Here's America Part Two: Haruki Murakami on Salinger, *The Great Gatsby*, and Why American Readers Sometimes Miss the Point." Interview by Roland Kelts. *A Public Space*, 1 (Spring 2006): 150–56.

"*Murakami Haruki shi eno jūgo no shitsumon* 村上春樹氏への１５の質問 (Fifteen Questions for Mr. Murakami Haruki)." Illustrations by Wada Makoto. *Kangaeru hito* 20 (Spring 2007): 30–39.

"'*Seichō' wo mezashite, nashitsuzukete: Murakami Haruki intabyū* 「成長」を目指して、成しつづけて——村上春樹インタビュー (Aiming at "Growth,' Keeping on Making: An Interview with Murakami Haruki)." Interview by Furukawa Hideo 古川日出男. *Monkey Business* 5 (Spring 2009): 4–78.

Yume wo miru tame ni maiasa boku wa mezameru no desu: Murakami Haruki intabyū shū 1997–2009 夢を見るために毎朝僕は目覚めるのです 村上春樹インタビュー集1997–2009 (*I Wake Up Every Morning to See a Dream: Murakami Haruki's Collected Interviews 1997–2009*). Bungei shunjū, 2010.

"*Murakami Haruki rongu intabyū* 村上春樹ロングインタビュー (A Long Interview with Murakami Haruki)." Interview by Matsuie Masashi 松家仁之. *Kangaeru hito* 33 (2010): 13–101.

Ozawa Seiji-san to, ongaku ni tsuite hanashi wo suru 小澤征爾さんと、音楽について話をする (*Talking about Music with Mr. Ozawa Seiji*). Shinchōsha, 2011.

Mimizuku wa tasogare ni tobitatsu: Kawakami Mieko kiku / Murakami Haruki kataru みみずくは黄昏に飛びたつ 川上未映子訊く / 村上春樹語る (*The Horned Owl Flies Off at Twilight: Kawakami Mieko Asks/Murakami Haruki Tells*). Shinchōsha, 2017.

ON TRANSLATION, WRITING, OR OTHER WRITERS

"<Dōjidai toshite no Amerika 5> toshi shōsetsu no seiritsu to tenkai: Chandorā to Chandorā ikō ＜同時代としてのアメリカ５＞都市小説の成立と展開――チャンドラーとチャンドラー以降 (<America as Contemporaneity 5> The Formation and Development of the City Novel: Chandler and after Chandler)." *Umi* 海 (May 1982): 198–207.

"Hon'yaku suru koto to, hon'yaku sareru koto 翻訳することと、翻訳されること (On Translating and Being Translated)." *Kokusai kōryū* 国際交流 73 (October 1996): 68–69.

Wakai dokusha no tame no tanpen shōsetsu annai 若い読者のための短編小説案内 (*A Guide to Short Stories for Young Readers*). Bungei shunjū, 1997.

Hon'yaku yawa 翻訳夜話 (*Informal Dialogues on Translation*). Cowritten with Shibata Motoyuki 柴田元幸. Bunshun shinsho 文春新書 129. Bungei shunjū, 2000.

"Kyacchā in za rai yakusha kaisetsu 『キャッチャー・イン・ザ・ライ』訳者解説 (The Translator's Comment on *The Catcher in the Rye*)." *Bungakukai* 57, no. 6 (2003): 263–83.

Hon'yaku yawa 2: Sarinjā senki 翻訳夜話２ サリンジャー戦記 (*Informal Dialogues on Translation 2: An Account of Struggle over Salinger*). Cowritten with Shibata Motoyuki. Bunshun shinsho 330. Bungei shunjū, 2003.

"Reimondo Cāvā, waga bungaku-teki dōkōsha レイモンド・カーヴァー、我が文学的同行者 (Raymond Carver, My Literary Companion)." *Chūō kōron* 中央公論 (September 2004): 226–30.

"Akutagawa Ryūnosuke: Downfall of the Chosen." Introduction to *Ryūnosuke Akutagawa: Rashōmon and Seventeen Other Stories*, translated by Jay Rubin, xix–xxxvii. London and New York: Penguin Books, 2006.

"Hon'yaku no kamisama 翻訳の神様 (The God of Translation)." Preface to *Murakami Haruki haibu・ritto* 村上春樹ハイブ・リット (*Murakami Haruki Hyb・rid*), 4–7. Aruku アルク, 2008.

"Herajika (Mūsu) wo otte へら鹿（ムース）を追って (In Chase of a Moose)." *Mystery Magazine* ミステリマガジン (May 2009): 32–34.

"Kaisetsu: mi wo konani shite shōsetsu wo kaku koto 解説――身を粉にして小説を書くこと (A Commentary: To Write Novels at the Expense of One's Being)." In Carol Sklenicka キャロル・スクレナカ, 2009, *Reimondo Cāvā: sakka toshite no jinsei* レイモンド・カーヴァー 作家としての人生 (*Raymond Carver: A Writer's Life*), translated by Hoshino Mari 星野真理, 726–36. Chūō kōron shinsha, 2013.

Shokugyō toshite no shōsetsuka 職業としての小説家 (*The Novelist as an Occupation*). Switch Publishing スイッチ・パブリッシング, 2015.

Murakami Haruki hon'yaku (hotondo) zen shigoto 村上春樹 翻訳（ほとんど）全仕事 (*Murakami Haruki: Translation (Almost) His Entire Work*). Chūō kōron shinsha, 2017.

Appendix 97

LIMITED-TERM COMPLETE WORKS

Murakami Haruki zen sakuhin 1979–1989 村上春樹全作品 1979–1989 (*The Complete Works of Murakami Haruki 1979–1989*). 8 vols. Kōdansha, 1990–1991.
Murakami Haruki zen sakuhin 1990–2000 村上春樹全作品 1990–2000 (*The Complete Works of Murakami Haruki 1990–2000*). 7 vols. Kōdansha, 2002–2003.

CORRESPONDENCE WITH READERSHIP VIA A TEMPORARY WEBSITE

CD-Rom-ban Murakami asahi-dō: yume no sāfu shitī CD-Rom版 村上朝日堂 夢のサーフシティー (*CD-Rom-Version Murakami Asahi Hall: The Dream Surf City*). Asahi shinbun sha, 1998.

"Sōda, Murakami-san ni kiite miyō" to seken no hitobito ga Murakami Haruki ni toriaezu buttsukeru 282 no daigimon ni hatashite Murakami-san wa chanto kotaerareru no ka? 「そうだ、村上さんに聞いてみよう」と世間の人々が村上春樹にとりあえずぶっつける282の大疑問に果たして村上さんはちゃんと答えられるのか？ (*Can Murakami-san Really Answer Well the 282 Large Questions People Throw at Him for Now When They Think, "Yes, Let's Ask Murakami-san"?*). Illustrations by Anzai Mizumaru. Asahi shinbun sha, 2000. Based on the *Murakami asahi-dō* homepage: http://opendoors.asahi-np.co.jp/span/asahido/index.htm, June–November, 1999.

CD-ROM-ban Murakami asahi-dō: Sumerujakofu tai Oda Nobunaga kashin-dan CD-ROM版 村上朝日堂 スメルジャコフ対織田信長家臣団 (*CD-Rom-Version Murakami Asahi Hall: Smerdyakov vs.* the Body of *Oda Nobunaga's Retainers*). Illustrations by Anzai Mizumaru. Asahi shinbun sha, 2001.

Kafka on the Shore Official Magazine: Murakami Haruki henshūchō: Shōnen Kafuka 村上春樹編集長 少年カフカ (*Murakami Haruki the Chief Editor: Kafka the Boy*). Shinchōsha, 2003. Based on the *Umibe no Kafuka* official homepage: Kafkaontheshore.com, September 12–November 20, 2002.

"Koredake wa Murakami-san ni itte okō" to seken no hitobito ga Murakami Haruki ni toriaezu buttsukeru 330 no shitsumon ni hatashite Murakami-san wa chanto kotaerareru no ka? 「これだけは村上さんに言っておこう」と世間の人々が村上春樹にとりあえずぶっつける330の質問に果たして村上さんはちゃんと答えられるのか？ (*Can Murakami-san Really Answer Well the 330 Questions People Throw at Him for Now When They Think, "I Want to Say THIS to Murakami-san?*). Illustrations by Anzai Mizumaru. Asahi shinbun sha, 2006. Based on the *Murakami asahi-dō* homepage: http://opendoors.asahi-np.co.jp/span/asahido/index.htm, June–November, 1999.

Murakami-san no tokoro 村上さんのところ (*Murakami-san's Place*). Illustrations by Fujimoto Masaru フジモトマサル. Shinchōsha, 2015. Based on the *Murakami-san no tokoro* homepage: www.welluneednt.com, January 15–May 13, 2015.

SPEECHES

"*Katarūnya kokusai-shō spīchi genkō zenbun* カタルーニャ国際賞スピーチ原稿全文 (The Entire Manuscript of the International Catalunya Prize Acceptance Speech)." Mainichi shinbun 毎日新聞. June, 2011. Accessed June 11, 2011. http://mainichi.jp/enta/art/news/20110611k0000m040017000c.html and http://mainichi.jp/enta/art/news/20110611k0000m040019000c.html.

"The Novelist in Wartime." The Jerusalem Prize Acceptance Speech. Salon.com. February 20, 2009. Accessed January 24, 2015. http://www.salon.com/2009/02/20/haruki_murakami/.

SELECT TRANSLATIONS INTO JAPANESE BY MURAKAMI

Allsburg, Chris Van. *Seifū-gō no sōnan* 西風号の遭難 (*The Wreck of the Zephyr*). Kawade shobō shinsha 河出書房新社, 1985.

Capote, Truman. *Tifanī de chōshoku wo* ティファニーで朝食を (*Breakfast at Tiffany's*). Shinchōsha, 2008.

Carver, Raymond. *Reimondo Cāvā zenshū* レイモンド・カーヴァー全集 (*The Complete Works of Raymond Carver*). Chūō kōron sha, 2004.

Chandler, Raymond. *Rongu guddobai* ロング・グッドバイ (*The Long Goodbye*). Hayakawa shobō 早川書房, 2010.

Crow, Bill. *Jazu anekudōtsu* ジャズ・アネクドーツ (*Jazz Anecdotes*). Shinchōsha, 2000.

Dyer, Geoff. *Batto byūtifuru* バット・ビューティフル (*But Beautiful*). Shinchōsha, 2011.

Fitzgerald, F. Scott. *Gurēto Gyattsubī* グレート・ギャッツビー (*The Great Gatsby*). Chūō kōron shinsha, 2006.

Fusilli, Jim. *Petto saunzu* ペット・サウンズ (*Pet Sounds*). Shinchōsha, 2008.

Gilmore, Mikal. *Shinzō wo tsuranukarete* 心臓を貫かれて (*Shot in the Heart*). Bungei shunjū, 1996.

Helprin, Mark. *Hakuchō-ko* 白鳥湖 (*Swan Lake*). Illustrations by Chris Van Allsburg. Kawade shobō shinsha, 1991.

Irving, John. *Kuma wo hanatsu* 熊を放つ (*Setting Free the Bears*). Chūō kōron sha, 1986.

Le Guin, Ursula K. *Sora tobi neko* 空飛び猫 (*Catwings*). Kōdansha, 1993.

Leonard, Elmore. *Onbure* オンブレ (*Hombre*). Shinchō bunko 新潮文庫, 2018.

McCullers, Carson. *Kekkonshiki no menbā* 結婚式のメンバー (*The Member of the Wedding*). Shinchō bunko, 2016.

Nichols, John. *Tamago wo umenai kakkō* 卵を産めない郭公 (*The Sterile Cuckoo*). Shinchō bunko, 2017.

O'Brien, William Timothy. *Hontō no sensō no hanashi wo shiyō* 本当の戦争の話をしよう (*The Things They Carried*). Bungei shunjū, 1990.

Paley, Grace. *Sono hi no gokoku ni* その日の後刻に (*Later the Same Day*). Bungei shunjū, 2017.
Salinger, J. D. *Kyacchā in za rai* キャッチャー・イン・ザ・ライ (*The Catcher in the Rye*). Hakusuisha 白水社, 2003.
Silverstein, Shel. *Ōkina ki* おおきな木 (*The Giving Tree*). Asunaro shobō あすなろ書房, 2010.
Solstad, Dag. *Noveru irebun, bukku eitīn* ノヴェル・イレブン、ブック・エイティーン (*Novel 11, Book 18 [Ellevte roman, bok atten]*). Chūō kōron shinsha, 2015.
Theroux, Marcel. *Kyokuhoku* 極北 (*Far North*). Chūō kōron shinsha, 2012.
Theroux, Paul. *Wāruzu endo* ワールズ・エンド (*World's End*). Bungei shunjū, 1987.

SELECT ANTHOLOGIES OF SHORT STORIES CHOSEN AND TRANSLATED BY MURAKAMI

Bāsudei sutōrīzu バースデイ・ストーリーズ (*Birthday Stories*). Chūō kōron shinsha, 2002.
Koishikute: Ten Selected Love Stories 恋しくて (*In Love: Ten Selected Love Stories*). Chūō kōron shinsha, 2013.

MURAKAMI'S WORKS TRANSLATED INTO ENGLISH

[In the order of publication in English]
A Wild Sheep Chase. Translated by Alfred Birnbaum. New York: Kodansha International, 1989.
Hard-Boiled Wonderland and the End of the World. Translated by Alfred Birnbaum. New York: Kodansha International and Kodansha America, 1991.
The Elephant Vanishes. Translated by Alfred Birnbaum and Jay Rubin. New York: Alfred A. Knopf, 1993. Containing "The Wind-Up Bird and Tuesday's Women," "The Second Bakery Attack," "The Kangaroo Communiqué," "On Seeing the 100% Perfect Girl One Beautiful April Morning," "Sleep," "The Fall of the Roman Empire, the 1881 Indian Uprising, Hitler's Invasion of Poland, and the Realm of Raging Winds," "Lederhosen," "Barn Burning," "The Little Green Monster," "Family Affair," "A Window," "TV People," "A Slow Boat to China," "The Dancing Dwarf," "The Last Lawn of the Afternoon," "The Silence," and "The Elephant Vanishes."
Dance Dance Dance. Translated by Alfred Birnbaum. New York: Kodansha America, 1994.
The Wind-Up Bird Chronicle. Translated by Jay Rubin. New York: Alfred A. Knopf, 1997.
South of the Border, West of the Sun. Translated by Philip Gabriel. New York: Alfred A. Knopf, 1999.

Norwegian Wood. Translated by Jay Rubin. New York: Vintage International, 2000.
Underground. Translated by Alfred Birnbaum and Philip Gabriel. London: Harvill Press, 2000.
Sputnik Sweetheart. Translated by Philip Gabriel. New York: Alfred A. Knopf, 2001.
After the Quake. Translated by Jay Rubin. New York: Alfred A. Knopf, 2002. Containing "UFO in Kushiro," "Landscape with Flatiron," "All God's Children Can Dance," "Thailand," "Super-Frog Saves Tokyo," and "Honey Pie."
Kafka on the Shore. Translated by Philip Gabriel. New York: Alfred A. Knopf, 2005.
Blind Willow, Sleeping Woman. Translated by Philip Gabriel and Jay Rubin. New York: Alfred A. Knopf, 2006. Containing "Blind Willow, Sleeping Woman," "Birthday Girl," "New York Mining Disaster," "Airplane: Or, How He Talked to Himself as If Reciting Poetry," "The Mirror," "A Folklore for My Generation: A Pre-History of Late-Stage Capitalism," "Hunting Knife," "A Perfect Day for Kangaroos," "Dabchick," "Man-Eating Cats," "A 'Poor Aunt' Story," "Nausea 1979," "The Seventh Man," "The Year of Spaghetti," "Tony Takitani," "The Rise and Fall of Sharpie Cakes," "The Ice Man," "Crabs," "Firefly," "Chance Traveler," "Hanalei Bay," "Where I'm Likely to Find It," "The Kidney-Shaped Stone That Moves Every Day," and "A Shinagawa Monkey."
After Dark. Translated by Jay Rubin. New York: Alfred A. Knoph, 2007.
What I Talk about When I Talk about Running. Translated by Philip Gabriel. New York: Alfred A. Knoph, 2008.
1Q84. Translated by Jay Rubin and Philip Gabriel. New York: Alfred A. Knoph, 2011.
Colorless Tsukuru Tazaki and His Years of Pilgrimage. Translated by Philip Gabriel. New York: Alfred A. Knoph, 2014.
Wind/Pinball: Hear the Wind Sing and Pinball, 1973 (Two Novels). Translated by Ted Goossen. New York: Alfred A. Knoph, 2015.
Absolutely on Music: Conversations with Seiji Ozawa. Translated by Jay Rubin. New York: Alfred A. Knoph, 2016.
Haruki Murakami Goes to Meet Hayao Kawai. Translated by Christopher Stephens. Einsiedeln: Daimon Verlag, 2016.
Men Without Women. Translated by Philip Gabriel and Theodore Goossen. New York: Alfred A. Knoph, 2017. Containing "Drive My Car," "Yesterday," "An Independent Organ," "Scheherazade," "Kino," "Samsa in Love," and "Men without Women."
Killing Commendatore. Translated by Philip Gabriel and Ted Goossen. New York: Alfred A. Knoph, 2018.

Bibliography

Anderson, Sam. "The Underground Man: The Fierce Imagination of Haruki Murakami." *The New York Times Magazine* 23 (October 2011): 36–41, 63.

Aoyama, Minami 青山南. "Murakami Haruki no 'Zō no shōmetsu' 村上春樹の「象の消滅」(Murakami Haruki's 'Elephant Vanishes')." 1994. In *Murakami Haruki*, edited by Komata, 237–253. Wakakusa shobō, 1998. Unless English translations are available, the translations of Japanese titles are mine. All the Japanese texts were published in Tokyo.

Baudrillard, Jean. "Simulacra and Simulations." 1981. In *Selected Writings*, translated by Paul Foss, Paul Patton, and Philip Beitchman; edited by Mark Poster, 169–187. 2nd edition. Stanford University Press: Stanford, 2001.

Benjamin, Walter. "The Work of Art in the Age of Its Technological Reproducibility." 1935–1936. In *The Work of Art in the Age of Its Technological Reproducibility, and Other Writings on Media*, translated by Edmund Jephcott and Harry Zohn. 2nd version. The Belknap Press of Harvard University Press: Cambridge, MA, 2008.

Freud, Sigmund. "The 'Uncanny.'" 1919. In *On Creativity and the Unconscious: Papers on the Psychology of Art, Literature, Love, Religion*, translated by Alix Strachey, 122–161. Harper & Row: New York, 1958.

Fukami, Haruka 深海遥. *Murakami Haruki no uta* 村上春樹の歌 (*Murakami Haruki's Songs*). Seikyūsha 青弓社, 1990.

Hisai, Tsubaki 久居つばき, and Kuwa Masato くわ正人. *Zō ga heigen ni kaetta hi: kīwādo de yomu Murakami Haruki* 象が平原に還った日: キーワードで読む村上春樹 (*The Day the Elephant Went Back to the Plain: Reading Murakami Haruki with Key Words*). Shinchōsha, 1991.

Hogle, Jerrold E. "Hyper-Reality and the Gothic Affect: The Sublimation of Fear from Burke and Walpole to *The Ring*." *English Language Notes* 48, no. 1 (Spring/Summer 2010): 163–176.

Ishikura, Michiko 石倉美智子. "*Fūfu no unmei I: 'Pan'ya saishūgeki' ron* 夫婦の運命I:「パン屋再襲撃」論 (The Fate of a Married Couple I: On 'The

Second Bakery Attack')." 1992. In *Murakami Haruki sutadīzu 2*, edited by Kuritsubo and Tsuge, 188–206. Wakakusa shobō 若草書房, 1999.

Jameson, Fredric. *Postmodernism, or, the Cultural Logic of Late Capitalism*. Duke University Press: Durham, 1991.

Katō, Norihiro 加藤典洋. *Bungaku chizu: Ōe to Murakami to nijūnen* 文学地図大江と村上と二十年 (*A Literary Map: Oe and Murakami and Twenty Years*). Asahi sensho 朝日選書 850. Asahi shinbun sha, 2008.

Kawai, Toshio 河合俊雄. "The Experience of the Numinous Today: Haruki Murakami." In *The Idea of the Numinous: Contemporary Jungian and Psychoanalytic Perspectives*, edited by Ann Casement and David Tacey, 186–199. Routledge: New York, 2006.

Kawakami, Chiyoko. "The Unfinished Cartography: Murakami Haruki and the Postmodern Cognitive Map." *Monumenta Nipponica* 57, no. 3 (Autumn 2002): 309–337.

Kawamoto, Saburō. "Kono karappo no sekai no naka de: Murakami Haruki ron この空っぽの世界のなかで: 村上春樹論 (In This Empty World: On Murakami Haruki)." 1991. In *Murakami Haruki*, edited by Komata, 7–29. Wakakusa shobō, 1998.

Kazamaru, Yoshihiko 風丸良彦. *Murakami Haruki tanpen saidoku* 村上春樹短編再読 (*Rereading Murakami Haruku's Short Stories*). Misuzu shobō みすず書房, 2007.

Kobayashi, Masaaki 小林正明. *Murakami Haruki: tō to umi no kanata ni* 村上春樹・塔と海の彼方に (*Murakami Haruki: Beyond the Tower and the Sea*). Shinwasha 森話社, 1998.

Komata, Tomoshi 木股知史, ed. *Murakami Haruki* 村上春樹. Nihon bungaku kenkyū ronbun shūsei 日本文学研究論文集成 46. Wakakusa shobō 1998.

Kuritsubo, Yoshiki 栗坪良樹. "Chinnyūsha TV pīpuru 闖入者TVピープル (TV People the Intruders)." In *Murakami Haruki sutadīzu* 3, edited by Kuritsubo and Tsuge, 274–284. Wakakusa shobō, 1999.

Kuritsubo, Yoshiki, and Tsuge Teruhiko 柘植光彦, eds. *Murakami Haruki sutadīzu 01-05* 村上春樹スタディーズ 1-5 (*Murakami Haruki Studies 1–5*). 5 vols. Wakakusa shobō, 1999.

Lacan, Jacques. *The Four Fundamental Concepts of Psycho-Analysis*. 1973. Translated by Alan Sheridan. Hogan Press: London, 1977.

Lyotard, Jean-François. *The Postmodern Condition: A Report on Knowledge*. 1979. Translated by Geoff Bennington and Brian Massumi. Theory and History of Literature 10. University of Minnesota Press: Minneapolis, 1984.

Matsui, Fumie 松井史絵. "*Hanpuku suru monogatari: 'Pan'ya saishūgeki' ron* 反復する物語:「パン屋再襲撃」論 (The Story That Repeats Itself: On 'The Second Bakery Attack')." In *Murakami Haruki to sen-kyūhyaku-hachijū nendai* 村上春樹と一九八〇年代 (*Murakami Haruki and the Nineteen-Eighties*), edited by Usami Takeshi 宇佐美毅 and Chida Hiroyuki 千田洋幸, 156–171. Ōfū おうふう, 2008.

Matsuoka, Kazuko 松岡和子. "Kyōfu no naka ni tenzai suru azayakana iro: Murakami Haruki cho 'TV pīpuru' 恐怖の中に点在する鮮やかな色: 村上春

樹著「TV ピープル」 (The Bright Colors Interspersed in Fear: 'TV People' by Murakami Haruki)." 1990. In *Murakami Haruki sutadīzu 3*, edited by Kuritsubo and Tsuge, 285–290. Wakakusa shobō, 1999.
Miller, J. Hillis. "The Critic as Host." *Critical Inquiry* 3, no. 3 (Spring 1977): 439–447.
Monnet, Livia. "Televisual Retrofutures and the Body of Insomnia: Visuality and Virtual Realities in the Short Fiction of Murakami Haruki." *Proceedings of the Midwest Association for Japanese Literary Studies*, no. 3 (1997): 340–380.
Mori, Mayumi 守真弓. "Murakami Haruki shi, sōsaku wa 'hitori kakifurai': Fukushima de kataru 村上春樹氏、創作 は 「一人 カ キ フ ラ イ」 福島で語る (Mr. Murakami Haruki, Creative Writing Is 'Solitary Oyster-Frying,' He Tells in Fukushima)." Asahi shinbun 朝日新聞. November 29, 2015. Accessed November 29, 2015. http://digital.asahi.com/articles/ASHCY5JD6HCYUCLV003.html?rm=520.
Morimoto, Takako 森本隆子. "'*Pan'ya saishūgeki*': hizai no na e mukete 「パン屋再襲撃」:非在の名へ向けて ('The Second Bakery Attack': Toward the Name of Nonexistence)." *Kokubungaku: kaishaku to kyōzai no kenkyū* 國文学:解釈と教材の研究 40, no. 4 (March 1995): 90–94.
Murakami, Haruki. *Yume de aimashō* 夢で会いましょう (*Let's Meet in Dreams*). Co-written with Itoi Shigesato. Tōjusha, 1981.
———. *Murakami asahi-dō* 村上朝日堂 (*The Murakami Asahi Hall*). Illustrations by Anzai Mizumaru. Wakabayashi Shuppan Kikaku, 1984.
———. *Pan'ya saishūgeki* パン屋再襲撃 (*The Second Bakery Attack*). Bungei shunjū, 1986.
———. *Murakami asahi-dō haihō!* 村上朝日堂 はいほー! (*The Murakami Asahi Hall Hi Ho!*). Bunka shuppan kyoku 文化出版局, 1989.
———. *Murakami Haruki zen sakuhin 1979–1989* 村上春樹全作品 1979–1989 (*The Complete Works of Murakami Haruki 1979–1989*). 8 vols. Kōdansha, 1990–1991.
———. *The Elephant Vanishes*. Translated by Alfred Birnbaum and Jay Rubin. Alfred A. Knopf: New York, 1993.
———. *Yagate kanashiki gaikokugo* やがて哀しき外国語 (*The Foreign Language That Makes Us Sad Before Long*). Kōdansha, 1994.
———. "*Hon'yaku suru koto to, hon'yaku sareru koto* 翻訳することと、翻訳されること (On Translating and Being Translated)." *Kokusai kōryū* 73 (October 1996): 68–69.
———. *The Wind-Up Bird Chronicle*. Translated by Jay Rubin. Alfred A. Knopf: New York, 1997a.
———. "Author Interviews: Haruki Murakami." Interview by Laura Miller and Don George. Salon.com, December 16, 1997b. Accessed December 10, 2014. http://www.salon.com/1997/12/16/int_2/.
———. *Hon'yaku yawa* 翻訳夜話 (*Informal Dialogues on Translation*). Co-written with Shibata Motoyuki. Bunshun shinsho 129. Bungei shunjū, 2000.

———. *Murakami Haruki zen sakuhin 1990–2000* 村上春樹全作品 1990–2000 (*The Complete Works of Murakami Haruki 1990–2000*). 7 vols. Kōdansha, 2002–2003.

———. *Hon'yaku yawa 2: Sarinjā senki* 翻訳夜話2 サリンジャー戦記 (*Informal Dialogues on Translation 2: An Account of Struggle over Salinger*). Co-written with Shibata Motoyuki. Bunshun shinsho 330. Bungei shunjū, 2003a.

———. "Haruki Murakami: écrire, c'est comme rêver éveillé." Interview by Minh Tran Huy. *Magazine Littéraire* 421 (June 2003b): 96–102.

———. "*Murakami Haruki rongu intabyū: Umibe no Kafuka wo kataru* 村上春樹ロング・インタビュー:『海辺のカフカ』を語る (A Long Interview with Murakami Haruki: Talking about *Kafka on the Shore*)." Interview by Yukawa Yutaka and Koyama Tetsurō. *Bungakukai* 文學界 57, no. 4 (April 2003c): 10–42.

———. "*Reimondo Cāvā, waga bungaku-teki dōkōsha* レイモンド・カーヴァー、我が文学的同行者 (Raymond Carver, My Literary Companion)." *Chūō kōron* (September 2004a): 226–230.

———. "Haruki Murakami: The Art of Fiction CLXXXII." Interview by John Wray. *The Paris Review* 170 (2004b): 115–151.

———. *Kafka on the Shore*. Translated by Philip Gabriel. Alfred A. Knopf: New York, 2005a.

———. "Sean Wilsey Talks with Haruki Murakami." In *The Believer Book of Writers Talking to Writers*, edited by Vendela Vida, 241–250. Believer Books: San Francisco, 2005b.

———. "*Murakami Haruki rongu intabyū: Afutā Dāku wo megutte* 村上春樹ロング・インタビュー:『アフターダーク』をめぐって (A Long Interview with Murakami Haruki: Concerning *After Dark*)." Interview by the Editing Office. *Bungakukai* 59, no. 4 (April 2005c): 172–193.

———. "'In Dreams Begins Responsibility': An Interview with Haruki Murakami." Interview by Jonathan Ellis and Mitoko Hirabayashi. *The Georgia Review* 59, no. 3 (Fall 2005d): 548–567.

———. "Akutagawa Ryūnosuke: Downfall of the Chosen." Introduction to *Ryūnosuke Akutagawa: Rashōmon and Seventeen Other Stories*, translated by Jay Rubin, xix–xxxvii. Penguin Books: London and New York, 2006a.

———. "Look Here's America Part Two: Haruki Murakami on Salinger, *The Great Gatsby*, and Why American Readers Sometimes Miss the Point." Interview by Roland Kelts. *A Public Space* 1 (Spring 2006b): 150–156.

———. "*Koredake wa Murakami-san ni itte okō" to seken no hitobito ga Murakami Haruki ni toriaezu buttsukeru 330 no shitsumon ni hatashite Murakami-san wa chanto kotaerareru no ka?* 「これだけは村上さんに言っておこう」と世間の人々が村上春樹にとりあえずぶっつける３３０の質問に果たして村上さんはちゃんと答えられるのか? (*Can Murakami-san Really Answer Well the 330 Questions People Throw at Him for Now When They Think, "I Want To Say THIS to Murakami-san?*)." Illustrations by Anzai Mizumaru. Asahi shinbun sha, 2006c. Based on the *Murakami asahi-dō* homepage: http://opendoors.asahi-np.co.jp/span/asahido/index.htm, June–November, 1999.

———. *Hashiru koto ni tsuite kataru tokini boku no kataru koto* 走ることについて語るときに僕の語ること (*What I Talk About When I Talk About Running*). Bungei shunjū, 2007a.

———. "*Murakami Haruki shi eno jūgo no shitsumon* 村上春樹氏への１５の質問 (Fifteen Questions for Mr. Murakami Haruki)." Illustrations by Wada Makoto. *Kangaeru hito* 20 (Spring 2007b): 30–39.

———. "*Hon'yaku no kamisama* 翻訳の神様 [The God of Translation]." Preface to *Murakami Haruki haibu・ritto* 村上春樹ハイブ・リット (*Murakami Haruki Hyb・rid*), 4–7. Aruku, 2008.

———. *Ichi-kyū-hachi-yon: bukku wan <shi-gatsu—roku-gatsu>* 1Q84: Book 1 ＜４月――６月＞ (*1Q84: Book 1 <April—June>*). Shinchōsha, 2009a.

———. "*Herajika (Mūsu) wo otte* へら鹿（ムース）を追って (In Chase of a Moose)." *Mystery Magazine* (May 2009b): 32–34.

———. "The Novelist in Wartime." The Jerusalem Prize Acceptance Speech. Salon.com. February 20, 2009c. Accessed January 24, 2015. http://www.salon.com/2009/02/20/haruki_murakami/.

———. "'*Seichō' wo mezashite, nashitsuzukete: Murakami Haruki intabyū*「成長」を目指して、成しつづけて――村上春樹インタビュー (Aiming at "Growth,' Keeping on Making: An Interview with Murakami Haruki)." Interview by Furukawa Hideo. *Monkey Business* 5 (Spring 2009d): 4–78.

———. *1Q84*. Translated by Jay Rubin and Philip Gabriel. Alfred A. Knopf: New York, 2011a.

———. "*Katarūnya kokusai-shō spīchi genkō zenbun* カタルーニャ国際賞スピーチ原稿全文 (The Entire Manuscript of the International Catalunya Prize Acceptance Speech)." *Mainichi shinbun* 毎日新聞. June, 2011b. Accessed June 11, 2011. http://mainichi.jp/enta/art/news/20110611k0000m040017000c.html and http://mainichi.jp/enta/art/news/20110611k0000m040019000c.html.

———. *Onna no inai otoko-tachi* 女のいない男たち (*Men Without Women*). Bungei shunjū, 2014.

———. *Shokugyō toshite no shōsetsuka* 職業としての小説家 (*The Novelist as an Occupation*). Switch Publishing, 2015.

———. *Mimizuku wa tasogare ni tobitatsu: Kawakami Mieko kiku / Murakami Haruki kataru* みみずくは黄昏に飛びたつ　川上未映子訊く／村上春樹語る (*The Horned Owl Flies Off at Twilight: Kawakami Mieko Asks/Murakami Haruki Tells*). Shinchōsha, 2017.

———. *Killing Commendatore*. Translated by Philip Gabriel and Ted Goossen. Alfred A. Knopf: New York, 2018.

———. "*Neko wo suteru: chichioya ni tsuite kataru tokini boku no kataru koto* 猫を棄てる―父親について語るときに僕の語ること (Abandoning a Cat: What I Talk About When I Talk About My Father)." *Bungei shunjū* 97, no. 6 (June 2019): 240–267.

Nakamura, Miharu 中村三春. "Yukue fumei no jinbutsu kankei: 'shōmetsu' to 'renkan' no monogatari 行方不明の人物関係:＜消滅＞と＜連環＞の物語 (The Relationship of Missing People: The Story of 'Disappearance' and 'Links')." *Kokubungaku: kaishaku to kyōzai no kenkyū* 43, no. 2 (1998): 104–110.

Nakata, Hideo 中田秀夫, dir. *Ringu* リング (*Ring*). 1998. 96 min. Tōhō 東宝, et al. Videocassette/DVD.

———, dir. *Ringu 2* リング 2 (*Ring 2*). 1999. 95 min. Tōhō, et al. Videocassette/DVD.

Parris, Michael. "*Ringu*: Japan and the Technological/Horrific Body." Conference paper, National Communication Association, 2007. 21p.

Phu, Thy. "Horrifying Adaptations: *Ringu*, *The Ring*, and the Cultural Contexts of Copying." *Journal of Adaptation in Film and Performance* 3, no. 1 (2010): 43–58.

Ragland-Sullivan, Ellie. *Jacques Lacan and the Philosophy of Psychoanalysis*. University of Illinois Press: Urbana and Chicago, 1986.

Rojas, Carlos. "Viral Contagion in the *Ringu* Intertext." In *The Oxford Handbook of Japanese Cinema*, edited by Daisuke Miyao, 416–437. Oxford University Press: Oxford, 2014.

Rubin, Jay. "The Other World of Murakami Haruki." *Japan Quarterly* 39, no. 4 (October-December, 1992): 489–500.

———. "*Zō no tsukurikata: Murakami Haruki wo yakushite* 象のつくり方: 村上春樹を訳して (How to Make an Elephant: On Having Translated Murakami Haruki)." *Kokusahi kōryū*, no. 73 (October 1996): 62–64.

Saitō, Tomoya 齋藤知也. "'*Shutai' eno kikyū: Murakami Haruki 'Zō no shōmetsu' ron* ＜主体＞への希求: 村上春樹「象の消滅」論 (A Longing for 'the Subject': On Murakami Haruki's 'Elephant Vanishes')." In *'Kyōshitsu' no naka no Murakami Haruki* ＜教室＞の中の村上春樹 (*Murakami Haruki in 'the Classroom'*), edited by Baba Shigeyuki 馬場重行 and Sano Masatoshi 佐野正俊, 75–93. Hitsuji shobō ひつじ書房, 2011.

Strecher, Matthew Carl. *Dances with Sheep: The Quest for Identity in the Fiction of Murakami Haruki*. Center for Japanese Studies at University of Michigan: Ann Arbor, MI, 2002.

Tanaka, Minoru 田中実. "*Kieteiku 'genjitsu': 'Naya wo yaku' sonogo 'Pan'ya saishūgeki'* 消えていく＜現実＞:「納屋を焼く」その後「パン屋再襲撃」 (The Vanishing 'Reality': 'Barn Burning' and Then 'The Second Bakery Attack')." 1990. In *Murakami Haruki*, edited by Komata, 184–195. Wakakusa shobō, 1998.

Wada, Atsuhiko 和田敦彦. "'*Zō no shōmetsu': zō wo meguru 'dokusha' no bōken* 「象の消滅」 象をめぐる＜読者＞の冒険 ('The Elephant Vanishes': The 'Reader's' Adventures Surrounding an Elephant)." *Kokubungaku: kaishaku to kyōzai no kenkyū* 43, no. 2 (February 1998): 159–163.

Wee, Valerie. "Visual Aesthetics and Ways of Seeing: Comparing *Ringu* and *The Ring*." *Cinema Journal* 50, no. 2 (Winter 2011): 41–60.

White, Eric. "Case Study: Nakata Hideo's *Ringu* and *Ringu 2*." In *Japanese Horror Cinema*, edited by Jay McRoy, 38–47. Edinburgh University Press: Edinburgh, 2005.

Yoshikawa, Yasuhisa 芳川泰久. *Murakami Haruki to Murakami Haruki: seishin bunseki suru sakka* 村上春樹とムラカミハルキ　精神分析する作家 (*Murakami Haruki and Murakami Haruki: The Psychoanalyzing Writer*). Mineruva shobō ミネルヴァ書房, 2010.

Yu, Eric K. W. "A Traditional Vengeful Ghost or the Machine in a Ghost? Narrative Dynamics, Horror Effects, and the Posthuman in *Ringu*." In *Fear Itself: Reasoning the Unreasonable*, edited by Stephen Hessel and Michèle Huppert, 109–124. Rodopi: Amsterdam, 2010.

Index

Abe, Kōbō, 10, 11, 73, 76n11; "*Chinnyūsha* (Intruders)," 76n11; *Friends*, 73
acrophobic, 31, 32, 34
After Dark, xiii
Agamemnon, 85
Akutagawa, Ryūnosuke, 7, 8, 9; "*Hana* (The Nose)," 8; "*Imogayu* (Yam Gruel)," 8; "*Kumo no ito* (The Spider's Thread)," 8, 10; "*Majutsu* (The Art of the Occult)," 8; "*To Shishun* (Tu Tze-chun)," 8
analogue TV, 57, 77, 78
an an magazine, 60
Anderson, Sam, 28
Angry Young Men, 86
antithesis. *See* thesis
Aomame, 50, 58, 71
Aoyama, Minami, 39
Apple desktop computer, 58

baby boomers, 2, 32
Barth, John, 16
Baudrillard, Jean, 66, 68–69; hyperspace, 68–69, 72; simulation/simulacra/ simulacrum, 66, 68–71, 73, 74, 78, 81
Beatles, 20
Benjamin, Walter, 66, 68, 72–73; authenticity, 72–73; technology of reproducibility, 66, 68, 72, 73

Big Macs, xvii, 25–27, 31. *See also* McDonald's
biotechnology, 44; biological experiment, 58. *See also* clone
Bluebird (car model), 37n12
Borges, Jorge Luis, 62; "The Aleph," 62; "The Garden of Forking Paths," 62
Bryan, C. D. B., 13

canon, xvi, 4, 9, 11, 12, 22, 34, 36n9, 87
capitalism, xvii, 4, 12, 23, 28, 37n10, 45, 51
Capote, Truman, 13
Carver, Raymond, xiii, 2, 13, 14, 16, 18n1; complete works of, xiv, 14; *What We Talk about When We Talk about Love*, 18n1
cassette tape, 57
Catalunya Prize. *See* International Catalunya Prize
CD-ROMs, xiv, 57
CDs, 13, 37n13, 53
cellular phones, 58
Chandler, Raymond, xiv, 13, 15, 17; *Farewell, My Lovely*, 17; *The Long Goodbye*, xiv, 13
children's stories, 11
clone, 58. *See also* biotechnology
collective unconscious. *See* Jung, Carl

109

Colorless Tsukuru and His Years of Pilgrimage, xiii
communism, 20, 23
consumerism, 27, 28, 35; consumables, 53, 60, 81; consumer items, goods or products, xv, xvii, 1, 26, 41, 59, 60, 70; consumer society, 60, 87; consuming, 26, 27, 48, 52, 82
Corolla, 28
Croissant magazine, 60
cyberspace, 77, 83, 84

Dance Dance Dance, xii, 60
"The Dancing Dwarf," 44, 54n9
Daphnis and Chloe, 9
Dazai, Osamu, 7, 8, 9; "*Hashire Merosu* (Run, Melos!)," 8, 10
DeLillo, Don, 16, 76n12; *White Noise*, 76n12
Descartes, René, 72
dialectic. *See* thesis
Disneyland, 68
Dolly the sheep, 58
Dostoevsky, Fyodor, xiv, 5, 14, 50; *The Brothers Karamazov*, 5, 36n10; *Demons*, 5; *Notes from Underground*, 50
DVD, 77
dystopian, 58

earthquake in 2011, xv, 55n19
East Asia, 3–4, 71
Edo Period, 3
efficiency, 19, 21, 25, 39, 44–48, 50, 52, 54n10, 68, 77
electronic book, 57
electronic media, xviii, 53, 57, 60, 69, 73, 75, 79, 80, 82, 87. *See also* televisual media
The Elephant Vanishes (book), xvii, 39, 53n1
"The Elephant Vanishes" (short story), xvii, 39–55, 87
Elle magazine, 60
Enlightenment, 72

family, xi, 63, 73, 85; family system, 73
Far East Network (FEN), 27
Fitzgerald, F. Scott, xiv, 13, 14; *The Great Gatsby*, xiv, 13
Frank O'Connor International Short Story Award, xv
Freud, Sigmund, 32, 33, 66–67, 79; castration-complex, 66; Freudian subconscious, 32; *heimlich*, 67; *id*, 79; repression, 66, 67, 68; *unheimlich*, 67. *See also Kafka on the Shore*; the uncanny
Fukami, Haruka, 19, 34

Gallagher, Tess, 18n1. *See also* Carver, Raymond
García Márquez, Gabriel, 62
Gilmore, Mikal, 13
Gothic, 79

Hans Christian Andersen Literature Award, xv
Hardboiled Wonderland and the End of the World, xii, xv, 43, 49, 51, 59, 71, 74; Calcutecs in, 74; Yamikuro in, 71
Hear the Wind Sing, xii, 2
Helprin, Mark, 13
Higuchi, Ichiyō, 10
Hisai, Tsubaki, and Kuwa Masato, 54n9, 55n16
Hogle, Jerrold E., 79

individualism, 73
information technology, 57, 59, 72
International Catalunya Prize, xiv, 52
Internet, 57, 58, 75, 75n3, 81, 83
Internet People, 83. *See also* Kuritsubo, Yoshiki
Irving, John, 13, 14, 16, 17
Ishiguro, Kazuo, 58; *Never Let Me Go*, 58
Ishikura, Michiko, 23, 24, 30, 32, 37n16

Jameson, Frederic, 27, 53, 72
Japanese culture, 2, 3, 12, 65

Japan-U.S. Security Treaty, xi, 20, 21, 25
Jerusalem Prize, xiv, xviii
Jung, Carl, 33; archetype, 33; collective unconscious, 33

Kafka, Franz, xiv, 2, 14, 40–42, 44, 50, 59; *The Castle*, 42; Franz Kafka Prize, xiv, 41; Gregor Samsa, 41; Kafkaesque, 22, 40; *The Metamorphosis*, 40, 41, 44; *The Trial*, 41
Kafka on the Shore, xii, xviii, 2, 5, 41, 49, 71; Hoshino in, 71; Oedipal desires in, 49
"The Kangaroo Communiqué," 57
katakana, 11, 68
Katei gahō magazine, 60
Katō, Norihiro, 21, 26, 36n7
Kawabata, Yasunari, 7, 8, 9, 10, 16; *Izu no odoriko* (*The Dancing Girl of Izu*), 8, 10
Kawai, Toshio, 19
Kawakami, Chiyoko, 40, 52, 53, 54n3
Kawamoto, Saburō, 51, 53
Kazamaru, Yoshihiko, 23, 36n5
Killing Commendatore, xiii, 58, 71, 75n3; Idea in, 71; Menshiki in, 58; Metaphor in, 71
Knoph, Alfred A., 53n1
Kobayashi, Masaaki, 25, 27, 32, 36n10
Kobe, xi, 2, 14
Kuritsubo, Yoshiki, 76n8, 76n11, 83

labyrinth, 62. *See also* maze
Lacan, Jacques, 33–35; big Other, 34; Imaginary, Symbolic and Real orders, 33–35; Lacanian unconscious, 33, 34
laptop, 58
Latin American literature, 4. *See also* South American writers
"Lederhosen," 54n13
Le Guin, Ursula K., 13
Lennon, John, 20, 26

LP records, xii, xiii, 23, 37n13, 53, 58, 64
Luddite, 63
Lyotard, Jean-François, 44, 53; performativity, 44–47

Macdonald, Ross (Kenneth Miller), 14; *The Name Is Archer*, 14
magic realism, 4, 19, 22, 29, 59, 62
majority principle, 73
Marie Claire magazine, 60
Marx, Karl, 20
Matsui, Fumie, 25, 27, 36n4, 36n5, 37n12, 37n16
Matsuoka, Kazuko, 79
maze, 62. *See also* labyrinth
McDonald's, xvii, 21, 25–26, 31, 48. *See also* Big Macs
Meiji Period, 73
Meiji Restoration, 7
Men Without Women, xiii, 18n2
"*Mikēne no shōwakusei hoteru* (The Little Planet Hotel in Mycenae)," 87n1
Miller, J. Hillis, 66, 70, 77, 81. *See also* paranormal
Mishima, Yukio, 2, 7, 8, 9, 16; *Shiosai* (*The Sound of Waves*), 9; *Yūkoku* (*Patriotism*), 36n9
Miyazawa, Kenji, 11; "*Amen nimo makezu*," 11; *Gingatetsudō no yoru* (*A Night on the Galaxy Railroad*), 11
modern, xiv, xv, 3, 4, 8, 9, 10, 13, 21, 23, 59, 63, 72, 73; modernization, 72
Monnet, Livia, 57, 61, 72, 74, 76n14
Mori, Mayumi, 54n15
Mori, Ōgai, 7, 8, 9; "*Maihime* (The Dancing Girl)," 8, 9; "*Sanshō dayū* (Sansho the Steward)," 8
Morimoto, Takako, 27, 36n5
Morris, Mary, 14
Morrison, Toni, 14
MTV, 60
Murakami, Yoko, xi, 85

Murasaki Shikibu, 10; *The Tale of Genji*, 10
music for Murakami, xiii–xiv, xvi, 1, 12
Mycenae, 85, 86

Nakamura, Miharu, 53n2, 54n4
Nakata, Hideo, 77, 82, 84n1. *See also Ringu*
Natsume, Sōseki, 7, 8, 9, 73; *Bocchan (Botchan)*, 8, 10; *Kokoro*, 73
Nobel Prize for Literature, xv, 10, 59
Norwegian Wood, xii, 2, 60
nuclear disaster, 11, 28, 52, 55n19. *See also* earthquake in 2011

Oates, Joyce Carol, 14
O'Brien, William Timothy, 13, 14, 16
Ōe, Kenzaburō, 2, 10–11
1Q84, xiii, xviii, 5, 21, 41–43, 50, 58, 71, 76n13; Ebisuno in, 76n13; Little People in, 71, 76n13
online, 57, 59, 75n1
Orpheus and Eurydice, 3
Orwell, George, 58, 76n13; Big Brother, 76n13; *Nineteen Eighty-Four*, 58
Ozawa, Seiji, xiv

Paley, Grace, 13, 14
pandemic, 82
"*Pan'ya shūgeki* (The Bakery Attack)," 19–23, 28–30
paranormal, 66, 70–72, 74, 77, 81, 83, 84
Parris, Michael, 81
performativity. *See* Lyotard, Jean-François
Peter Cat, xii
Phu, Thy, 80
Pinball, 1973, xii
Petite Planète, La, 85
Playboy magazine, 55n16
posthuman, 75
postindustrial, 19, 40, 52
postmodern, 3–4, 16, 56, 61, 72, 74, 75, 76n12, 82

post-World War II. *See* World War II
premodern, 3, 71
Princeton University, xii, xiv, xv, 14
Pynchon, Thomas, 16

Ragland-Sullivan, Ellie, 37n18
realistic, 16, 42, 58, 59, 87
Reed, Lou, 60
Ringu, xviii, 77–84, 84n1; Sadako in, 78–79, 81–84
Ringu 2, 83
Rohas, Carlos, 84n2
Rubin, Jay, 7, 53, 53n1, 54n3
running by Murakami, xiii, xvi, 12, 17, 86

Sadako 3D, 84
Saitō, Tomoya, 43, 54n12
Salinger, J. D., xiv, 13; *The Catcher in the Rye*, xiv, 13
Samsa, Gregor. *See* Kafka, Franz
Sarin nerve gas attack. *See Underground*
Schelling, Fredrich Wilhelm Joseph, 67
science fiction, 58
The Second Bakery Attack (book), xiii, xvii, 19, 39, 42
"The Second Bakery Attack" (short story), xvi, 19–37, 39, 48, 54n14, 87; cavern in, 30–32, 33, 34, 35; submarine volcano in, 30–35, 48
seismic. *See* earthquake in 2011
self, 32, 33, 48; dismantlement of, 57, 72–74
Shiga, Naoya, 7, 8, 9; "*Kozō no kamisama* (Shopboy's God)", 8
Shimazaki, Tōson, 7–9
Shokugyō toshite no shōsetsuka (The Novelist as an Occupation), 1
Shōnen Kafuka (Kafka the Boy), 75n1
Sillitoe, Alan, 86; *The Loneliness of the Long-Distance Runner*, 86
Silverstein, Shel, 13
"Sleep," 26
smartphones, 58

sōgō shōsetsu (comprehensive novel), 5
SONY, 27, 63, 67
South American writers, 62
South of the Border, West of the Sun, xii, 43
Sputnik Sweetheart, xiii, 2, 43
Strand, Mark, 13
Strecher, Matthew Carl, 21
surveillance, 58, 74, 81
synthesis. *See* thesis
system, xi, xiv, 4, 20, 27, 33, 34, 41, 57, 58, 62, 76n7, 77, 83; against the, xiv, xvii, xviii, 14, 28, 40, 52–53, 86, 87; being part of the, 23, 25–27, 40, 53, 63; system language, 2, 34; TV system, 57, 61, 74, 75, 81, 83. *See also* family, family system

Tanaka, Minoru, 27, 36n5, 37n14
Tanizaki, Jun'ichirō, 7, 9; *Sasameyuki (The Makioka Sisters)*, 9, 10
technology of communication, 58, 73, 77. *See also* information technology
technophobia, 61
televisual media, 75, 77, 79. *See also* electronic media
televisual space, 68, 70, 78
Theater of the Absurd, 10
Theroux, Paul, 13
thesis, xii, 20, 29, 30; antithesis, 29; dialectic, 29; synthesis, 26, 29
tsunami. *See* earthquake in 2011
Tufts University, xiv, xv, 14
TV People (book), xiii, xvii
"TV People" (short story), xvii, xviii, 24, 39, 42, 48, 49, 53, 57–84, 87

Ueda, Akinari, 3; *Ugetsu monogatari (The Tales of Rain and Moon)*, 3
"UFO in Kushiro," 37n15
the uncanny, 66–68, 72, 74
Underground, xiv
United Red Army, 21

U.S.-Japan Security Treaty. *See* Japan-U.S. Security Treaty

Van Allsburg, Chris, 13
videotape, 78, 79, 81, 83; VHS, 78; videocassette, 77, 80; video copies multiplied, 82

Wada, Atsuhiko, 39, 40, 44, 45, 54n4, 54n10
Wagner, Richard, 20, 22–23, 34, 36n9; *The Flying Dutchman*, 23; *Tannhaüser*, 23; *Tristan and Isolde*, 22, 36n9
Waseda University, xi
websites by Murakami, 12
Wee, Valerie, 80
a well, 49, 78, 79; *ido*, 79
Welt Literature Award, xv
What I Talk about When I Talk about Running, xiii, 2, 13, 18n1
White, Eric, 80
white noise, 74
A Wild Sheep Chase, xii, 2, 24, 46, 49, 74; Boss's secretary in, 46; star-marked sheep in, 74
"The Wind-Up Bird and Tuesday's Women," 54n15
The Wind-Up Bird Chronicle, xii, xviii, 5, 24, 44, 49, 53n2, 54n15, 57, 62, 74, 76n7; Hsin-ching in, 44; Okada Toru in, 49; Wataya Noboru in, 74
The Wizard of Oz, 26
women as mediums, 37n17, 47
World Fantasy Award, xv
World War II, xi, 32, 44, 58, 73; post-World War II, 13, 52, 86
World Wide Web, 84

Yakult Swallows, xii
Yoshikawa, Yasuhisa, 37n11
Yu, Eric K. W., 80

About the Author

Masaki Mori received his B.A. and M.A. degrees in English from Tohoku University before his Ph.D. in Comparative Literature from the Pennsylvania State University in 1990. He has publications on Kawabata Yasunari, Murakami Haruki, Asian-American literature, and the epic tradition as well as pedagogic topics. He is currently associate professor and head of the Department of Comparative Literature and Intercultural Studies at the University of Georgia. He also directs five Asian language programs.

www.ingramcontent.com/pod-product-compliance
Lightning Source LLC
Chambersburg PA
CBHW020127010526
44115CB00008B/1018